I Just Wanna Be Me!

BY ELIZABETH WAKES

I Just Wanna Be Me!

Trilogy Christian Publishers

A Wholly Owned Subsidiary of Trinity Broadcasting Network

2442 Michelle Drive, Tustin, CA 92780

Copyright © 2024 by Elizabeth Wakes

All Scripture quotations are taken from the King James Version of the Bible. Public domain.

All rights reserved, including the right to reproduce this book or portions thereof in any form whatsoever.

For information, address Trilogy Christian Publishing

Rights Department, 2442 Michelle Drive, Tustin, Ca 92780.

Trilogy Christian Publishing/ TBN and colophon are trademarks of Trinity Broadcasting Network.

For information about special discounts for bulk purchases, please contact Trilogy Christian Publishing.

Trilogy Disclaimer: The views and content expressed in this book are those of the author and may not necessarily reflect the views and doctrine of Trilogy Christian Publishing or the Trinity Broadcasting Network.

10 9 8 7 6 5 4 3 2 1

Library of Congress Cataloging-in-Publication Data is available.

ISBN 979-8-89333-463-0

ISBN 979-8-89333-464-7 (ebook)

Dedication

I want to dedicate this book to my father, Raymond, and my mother, Ida, for their many prayers and their dedication to God. They are both watching on me from heaven. My father and my mother both have a great testimony. When my father got saved, he was constantly in the Word of God and in prayer. He would pray three times a day without fail, and he carried his Bible everywhere that he went. He was a man of great faith, and he was fearless in the face of the devil! He would witness to anyone that he would meet, and many lives were changed because of it.

My sweet, beautiful mother was a woman of faith, love, and wisdom. She was always quiet when others would talk, and no one knew that she was secretly reading them. She raised us up in the fear of the Lord. She also loved reading the Bible. Because of their dedication to God, I am who I am today, and I can't wait to see them!

Table of Contents

Introduction..7

Chapter 1: Starting Over...9

Chapter 2: No Pain, No Gain...13

Chapter 3: And You Shall Know the Truth.....................19

Chapter 4: Let Patience Have Her Perfect Work............27

Chapter 5: What Is the Church?..33

Chapter 6: Sons and Daughters of God............................47

Chapter 7: Nothing Shall Separate Me from the Love of God.....63

Chapter 8: The Fear of the Lord Is Only the Beginning...............71

Chapter 9: Put Not Your Trust in Man............................83

Chapter 10: Freedom from People's Opinions................89

Chapter 11: The Lord Is My Shepherd; I Shall Not Want............95

Chapter 12: Think on These Things.................................99

Chapter 13: Pride of Life..103

Chapter 14: Casting Down Imaginations.......................111

Chapter 15: Seek First the Kingdom of God..................117

Chapter 16: God's Ways Are Higher..............................121

Chapter 17: Without Faith It's Impossible....................127

Chapter 18: Love Your Neighbor as Yourself...............133

Chapter 19: The Lust of the Eyes..141

Chapter 20: The Effects of Words..147

Chapter 21: Pruning Is a Must!..153

Chapter 22: Daddy Chastises...159

Chapter 23: For All Have Sinned and Come Short.......................165

Chapter 24: There Is Power in the Word......................................175

Chapter 25: There Is Freedom in Forgiveness.............................179

The Conclusion..185

Introduction

I have no great introduction to give as many great authors may have, nor have I accomplished any great achievements to talk about. My father and mother have taken me to church most of my life, and though they did their best for me, after I had attended church for so long, I still did not know God, and I strayed. Later in life, God found me!

Many years ago, when I first gave my life to God, God made Himself known to me. I wasn't attending church at the time, nor was I hanging around Christians when I got saved. I believe that through my parents' prayers, God showed up in my life. One day, I was staying at this beautiful hotel overlooking the beach, and when I woke up, I saw Jesus. He was sitting on a chair at the foot of my bed.

He was wearing a white robe. He had His hands on His face, and He was crying uncontrollably. I asked Him what was wrong, and He responded, "So many people are going to hell!" I started crying, and I told Him that I was sorry and that I wished that I could help Him. I also told Him that I didn't know what to do and that I didn't know anything about the Bible. I felt helpless!

God has appeared to me several times in my life before and after I got saved. And before I truly got saved, I didn't really like God because of what I heard about Him at church. I would tell God that when I saw Him, I was going to give Him a piece of my mind because when He created me, He knew that I was created to go to hell! I told Him that He knew that I could not live by His rules! I was taught religion! I was taught that anything fun, such as bowling, movies, skating, ballgames, and watching television, was all evil and would send me straight to hell!

I am here to say that I've learned there is so much more that God has to offer to Christians. Religion is not a system that people follow, but it is having a best friend who understands everything that you are going through and who will always be by your side through thick and thin! For many years I believed that I was experiencing a relationship with Jesus until one day I realized that I didn't even know Him. I was just going through the motions, and I was not experiencing the things that God wanted me to experience.

I believe that I can help now. I wrote this book years ago, and as much as I wanted to get it published, I know that it was not God's timing. Now is the time! I am not looking for fame, as you will read in my book, but I am looking to help others reach higher heights with God. Everything that I do, I want it to be a blessing for my King!

What I am writing for you to read is what I have experienced, and it has gotten me so close to God. I can tell you that I know that without a shadow of a doubt, God directs my every step and everything that happens in my life is ordained by Him.

God is more real to me than anything around me. If you feel that you are missing something in your life, and if you feel that you know that there is so much more to God than what you are experiencing, I believe that this book will give you the answers that you have been looking for to change your life and be the person that God has created you to be!

Chapter 1

Starting Over

Before I started writing this book, I had just finished writing another book. I wrote it about three years before I wrote this book, and I really thought that it was going to be a big hit! The book that I wrote contained five hundred and thirty pages. The pages of that book were filled with things that happened to me in the three years that it took me to write that book. It was basically about what I was going through in those three years.

I had read through that book a couple of times, but when I started reading it for the third time then I began erasing a lot of the pages that I felt should not be in that book. After reading it through for the third time, I got so tired of reading it, and I got so frustrated because I couldn't seem to find the titles of chapters, and it seemed like everything was out of place! Then I realized that my book was just a big mess!

After reading it for the third time, I realized that it was not a book, but it was more like my diary. Most of the book was about the pain and suffering that I was going through while I was going through a fiery trial. I had gone through such devastation in my life, and it just seemed like the pain would never ever ever ever end, and this went on for three whole long years of my life!

Now I don't feel that I need to talk about how much pain I went through in this book; that's because I can say that I have finally been healed from the pain that I had been feeling for so very long. So I decided to write another book while I'm in my right mind and without me feeling all that miserable pain.

I can honestly say that I have been healed from five hundred and thirty pages worth of pain and suffering, and I can rejoice because that pain is completely gone! I am free! Thank You, Jesus, for sending Your Word and healing me! I can say that that pain and suffering that I had gone through has brought me so much closer to my Jesus than ever before, and that right there is worth every bit of what I went through.

While I was going through this trial, I tried to get help from other people, but I couldn't seem to find anyone to talk to but my Jesus. *He was there all the time waiting ever so patiently!* The thing is that before I had gone through such devastation in my life with this trial, I really believed that I was saved and on my way to heaven. I really believed that everything was A-okay, and I believed that I was a good Christian because I did everything that a Christian person did. I attended church faithfully, I volunteered, I paid my tithes, and I jumped and danced and hollered really, really loud, and on top of that, I even had a title!

But God was wonderful enough to allow me to go through everything that I went through so that He could get my attention and get me on the right path because I definitely was not! At first, I couldn't understand why so many bad things were happening to me, but after I had my fits and screamed like a crazy woman, and after I threw my tantrums, and when I couldn't cry one more tear or say one more word, God started to speak to me. I can truly say that I heard Him speak loud and clear.

So instead of me telling you five hundred and thirty pages of what I had gone through and instead of going through the details of how bad I was feeling and instead of me writing about the horrible experience that I faced, I would rather write a book that talks about how I got closer to God. I would much rather speak about how my God has brought me through this. "Weeping may endure for a night, but joy cometh in the morning" (Psalm 30:5). I can say that when you truly know God, then His joy will come.

What I want to talk about is how I got saved for real. Through this experience I was able to find out just how real God is, and not only that, but God has been teaching me how to really be saved. I have read several good books, and I can say that none of them were even close to five hundred and thirty pages either! TMI! Way too much!

Even though I spent a lot of time writing that five-hundred-and-thirty-page book, I don't feel that I wasted my time because as I wrote down what I was going through, I feel like I was able to release what I was feeling. And as I read through that book for the third time, I was able to see just how I was really feeling through those long, miserable years, and I was also able to see what God has faithfully brought me through.

And the really great thing is that even though I went through a storm with crashing waves that I never believed that I would survive, nor did I think that nightmare would ever end because it just didn't seem possible, but now I know that I know that I know that all things really are possible with God! So I started writing a new book all over again.

Chapter 2

No Pain, No Gain

The trial that I was going through was very painful for me. I don't believe that I had ever experienced that kind of pain for that long of a time before. The reason that I wept so much was that what I went through had dealt with so many people that I loved and I was hurt by; some of these people I had trusted with my life and my soul.

It was my fault because I believed that some of these people were perfect and that they could never make any mistakes. I took every word that they said as pure gold, and I have to say that God didn't like that one bit! When you love someone, you really want to trust them and believe in them, but with all that I have been through, I'm actually finding out why the scripture tells us not to put our trust in man. "Put not your trust in princes, nor in the son of man, in whom there is no help" (Psalm 146:3).

It took a while for me to understand that scripture. People want to believe in other people, and we want someone whom we can really, really trust and even depend on, but through this trial, I learned that everyone is flawed and that no one knows everything. I've also learned that some people who act like they are so smart don't know anything. Too many people are chasing after men and women for their help. Some look for a husband, some look for a wife, and some look for powerful anointed preachers to follow.

Many people believe that they need to find the right person so that they can get the help or the answers that they may need, or they just may be looking to get the fulfillment that they feel they may need. I thought I really found what I was missing in certain people, and I really felt that my life was perfect when I met them. I felt that I had everything in my life that I needed to help me to be "the Christian" that I was supposed to be. It wasn't until I had gone through this trial that I realized what was really missing for me to be the real Christian: the One True God.

I had put my trust in people who I believed had a perfect life and who could do no wrong, but I learned all right! We must understand that nobody is perfect! When I saw the people who I felt were perfect do imperfect things, I totally freaked out! I couldn't believe what I had heard or what I was seeing, and I honestly felt like I had just entered in the "twilight zone!" To me this pain that I was feeling was kind of like a woman who would find her husband in bed with another woman.

It just seemed like everyone whom I put my trust in for whatever reason had failed me miserably and my heart was crushed because of it. I can honestly say that I have learned the true meaning of pain. This pain that I felt literally felt like a knife had been jabbed in me and it was left in me for years! I had felt that heart-throbbing, stabbing pain and every single day! The knife seemed to be twisting every way, and it just wouldn't stop twisting! This went on for three years of my life!

Every day I woke up feeling that way! What's crazy is that no matter what I did, I couldn't stop feeling that pain, and believe me, I tried everything and anything! I knew that it was time to really try *Jesus*! There were days that I wanted so badly to get drunk, but I knew that wouldn't help me. So I made the decision to call on *God*, the One that I really thought that I knew; like I said, there was no one else to call.

I was taking care of my mom at the time, and then on top of that, she got very sick, and that was just another pain added to my pain. My mother lived with me for over twenty-five years, and I took good care of her. She had such a pure heart. I spoiled her rotten, and I made sure that she got whatever her heart desired! I love and miss her so very much!

The one thing that was so very hard for me to do was to watch my mom suffer because when she would suffer, I would feel her pain. She had fallen a couple of times, and one time she broke her ribs, and another time she broke her arm. When my mom would suffer, I would get hysterical and basically lose my mind! At one point she started to lose her memory, and for me to watch that made me even more hysterical!

Anytime that my mom would get sick, I would get so frantic, and I would go to my garage, which is detached from my house, and I would have myself crying fits. When I say that I went hysterical, I mean just that! One day while I was having my fit in the garage, I was crying out to God, telling Him that He couldn't take my mom from me, and I heard God in an audible voice say, "I'll take her if I want to!" He went on to say, "She ain't yours, she's mine, and I will take her if I want!" It was like someone had just slapped me in the face! I must say that I snapped out of it! After that my mom got better, and she regained her memory. Even as my mom got older, she always had a sharp memory.

As I was going through this trial, I tried to figure out what pain was about. "Analyze this!" I thought that if I tried to do that, then maybe the pain wouldn't feel so bad, but it didn't work! It didn't make the pain feel any less painful whatsoever! And after a few days of crying my head off, I told God that I wanted to be closer to Him and that I wanted to walk after the Spirit and be His child.

I cried that prayer for many days. I always held my Bible close to me when I prayed; I guess I felt that if I held the Bible close to me, I was close to Him. But one day while I was crying out, I heard God speak in an audible voice saying, "Read the Bible." The first time I heard God say that I ignored Him and just kept crying and holding the Bible close to me and telling Him that I wanted to be so close to Him.

And the next day, as I was telling Him that I wanted to be so close to Him, I heard God say it again, "Read the Bible." The second time He repeated it, I still ignored Him and kept crying. The third day I cried out to Him again, telling Him I wanted to be close to Him, and the third time He spoke again, "You have to read the Bible!" Then I heard Him say, "Open the Bible and read it!" and then He said, "It's all there in the Book!" And that was when I started to read the Bible through from the beginning to the end. My brother gave me a One Year Bible and it tells us what to read each day; it gives us chapters to read from the Old Testament and chapters from the New Testament so that we can read it through in a year.

I had read through the Bible a couple of times many years earlier, and I used to love reading the Bible, but as time passed, I slowly stopped reading it. Then after a while, I really didn't know what to read. So, when I would have time to read it, I would just open up the Bible and read anything. You know, like you often hear people say, "Lord, whatever I open the Bible to read, it must be from You." And sadly, that's what some people actually go by when they read the Bible, but they are missing so much.

I had gotten so involved with the church that I really didn't have a lot of time to pray or read my Bible like I once used to. I loved my church so much. I guess the reason that I loved it so much was because, for the first time, I felt like I was accepted at a church, and I felt loved. For the first time, I felt respected at a church, but the problem was that I started loving the church more than God. I became an idol worshipper of my church by giving all my time to the ministry and very little time to God, and God got jealous! "For thou shalt not worship no other god: for the Lord, whose name is Jealous, is a jealous God" (Exodus 34:14).

So, after I started reading the Bible through, I began to read things in the Bible that I never heard preached on any pulpit. One thing that freaked me out was that there were so many scriptures that say suffering is in order! Excuse me? When I read 2 Corinthians 4:17, "For our light affliction, which is but for a moment, worketh for us a far more exceeding and eternal weight of glory," and when I read Romans 8:18, "For I reckon that the sufferings of this present time are not worthy to be compared with the glory which shall be revealed in us." I must say that made me feel a little better about suffering.

After I read those verses, I began relating my sufferings to a pregnant woman who knows that she is going to suffer through her pregnancy and delivery. She's okay with suffering because she knows that her reward will be great! But I have to say those scriptures still didn't make my pain feel any less painful. Just like a pregnant woman who knows about the pain that she will suffer won't make her labor pains feel any less painful.

But I can honestly say that the result that I have experienced after going through the pain is great! I can say that all my pain and suffering brought forth great intimacy with my Jesus, and I know that I know that I know my Redeemer lives! I know that my suffering brought forth something great that cannot be compared to what I have suffered. And now I know that I know that I can only put my trust in God! He let me know that He is the only *perfect* One! God showed me that man will surely fail me, but He never will! Amen!

I love the song by Andraé Crouch "Through It All" because I can definitely relate to it! I've had tears, I've had questions, and I definitely had storms, but God is faithful and has brought me through them all!

Chapter 3

And You Shall Know the Truth

When I began reading the Bible and I got to the book of Revelation, I read the part that says all liars go to the lake of fire. "But the fearful, and unbelieving, and the abominable, and murderers, and whoremongers, and sorcerers, and idolaters, and all liars, shall have their part in the lake which burneth with fire and brimstone: which is the second death" (Revelation 21:8). "Then I remembered reading the scripture that says that the devil is the father of lies" (John 8:44). I must say that I was totally in shock!

It was like a bright shining light flashed in my face! At the time, I was running a business, and when a customer would call me to reserve my product (I rented out inflatable bounces), there were a lot of times that I would lie to them. I lied because I wanted them to use my company. I would tell them that we had the best products, and I would tell them that they needed to book quickly because we were booking fast. I would tell customers just about anything just to get a sale.

I would also lie to my mother, and I would also tell other people to lie to her as well! The reason that I would tell them to lie to her was because I didn't want her to hear any bad news. I wanted so badly to protect her from getting down. At the time, she had high blood pressure, so I was worried that her blood pressure would go up sky-high if she heard any bad news, so I would only tell her good things even if it was a lie.

One year, one of my sisters died, and I refused to tell my mother because I knew how it would make her feel. I fought with some of my family members who felt that she should know. My mom rarely saw my sister who passed, and I figured that since she hardly ever saw her, she didn't need to know that she passed. But then I realized that she would eventually find out and she wouldn't be happy with me when she did, so I decided to let them tell her the truth.

So, when I realized how much of a big, fat liar I was, I went to God and told Him that I was going to go to hell—like He didn't already know that! The Bible says, "Lying lips are abomination to the Lord: but they that deal truly are his delight" (Proverbs 12:22). We are either going to believe that the Bible is true or believe that it's not. I choose to *believe* every word of the Bible.

At the time, I really felt like it was impossible for me to stop lying. I know so many people who call themselves Christians lie all the time and don't think anything about it, as I didn't…until I saw the light! So I really didn't know what I was going to do. I would lie to everybody, and I just couldn't help it! I remember how I had to stop talking to people just so I wouldn't lie. That's how bad it was!

So, when I asked God to help me stop lying, guess what? He did! After a while, I began noticing that I was lying a lot less compared to how I used to lie. I have to say that this was by far one of the hardest things for me to do! So instead of lying to my mom, I started telling her the truth no matter how I felt that it would affect her. I just knew that I couldn't lie anymore.

When I told my mom that my sister had died, she reacted as any mother would react to her daughter's death, but she didn't act the way that I thought that she would when she heard the news. At that time, she was on high blood pressure pills, and I forgot to give her blood pressure pills that day! So, once again, I was losing it, but I was shocked to see that she was fine. I realized that I was the crazy one!

And what's crazy is when I started telling my mom the truth about other things, no matter how bad of news it was, to my surprise, she did not react the way that I expected her to. Of course, she wasn't happy about the bad news, but she didn't go crazy and get sick over what I told her the way that I had thought that she would. I would always keep an eye on her to make sure of that.

After I saw how she reacted to bad news, I realized that I had carried so much weight by holding so much inside of me! On top of that, I would go crazy trying to figure out how to make sure that no one else would give her bad news! That was even more weight on my shoulders! I remember whenever someone would call my mom, how I would try and listen to their conversation and try to make sure that they wouldn't give her bad news. Do you know how hard that was?

But when I realized how coocoo I was acting and how much time I wasted on trying to protect my mom from hearing the truth, let's just say it hurts when I think about it! I also noticed that the more that I started telling the truth, the freer I began to feel. I can now say that God has delivered me from a lying spirit, but once again God has proved to me that "all things are truly possible with God!" (Matthew 19:26).

One thing that I realized was that for me to live a lie was to live in complete darkness because God's Word is truth. When a person is living a lie, they, too, are walking in darkness, and they really cannot see. "Jesus saith unto him, I am the way, the truth, and the life: no man cometh unto the Father, but by me" (John 14:6). Only truth will set us free!

What's really sad is when I hear preachers who don't preach the absolute truth about what the Bible says and its totality. They will use parts of certain scriptures and leave out the rest of them so they can tickle the crowd's ears, and some of them just right out lie. There are so many things that I am reading in the Bible now that people need to hear so that they can grow spiritually, but not many preachers seem to preach about.

There are so many people who are following preachers and believing everything that they are preaching as I found myself doing. And there are many followers who will live by the revelation that other preachers get instead of seeking God to get their own revelation. If preachers started preaching everything that's in the Bible today, they would probably be shunned by their congregation and shunned by many preachers, just like the prophets of old were.

Nowadays, it sounds weird for people to call evil, evil and good, good. We don't judge here! God loves everybody no matter what they do. Though God does love everybody, and He showed it by sending His Son to die for everyone, the Bible says that it's not God's will that any man perish. "The Lord is not slack concerning his promise, as some men count slackness; but is longsuffering to us-ward, not willing that any should perish, but that all should come to repentance" (2 Peter 3:9).

In that same chapter God is warning the people to be diligent and walk in His peace, without spot and blameless. "Wherefore, beloved, seeing that ye look for such things, be diligent that ye may be found of him in peace, without spot, and blameless" (2 Peter 3:14). The fact is God loves us enough to change us. He wants to bring us out of darkness into His light.

"But ye are a chosen generation, a royal priesthood, an holy nation, a peculiar people; that ye should shew forth the praises of him who hath called you out of darkness into his marvellous light" (1 Peter 2:9). God sent His Son to die for us so that we can have the opportunity to become His child, to become His sons and daughters.

The Bible also says those who reject God, He will also reject them, and He will laugh at their calamity (Proverbs 1:26). I know that this sounds harsh, but nevertheless, it's God's Word. In the book of Deuteronomy, chapter 28 tells us what God will do to those who disobey Him and what He does to those who obey Him. And if you read through the Old Testament, you will read about all the horrible things that God has done to those who disobeyed Him. If you read the bad part of Deuteronomy 28, you will see that it is pretty much what is happening in the world today.

Sadly, many preachers think that God has changed, and they believe that God doesn't punish people for being disobedient. God's Word says that He chastises those He loves. Not too long ago, I heard one well-known preacher say that some of the words spoken by Jesus are not for us because he felt that we could not obey something that Jesus said. "Every word of God is pure: he is a shield unto them that put their trust in him. Add thou not unto his words, lest he reprove thee, and thou be found a liar" (Proverbs 30:5–6).

Another well-known preacher preached from the pulpit saying that eighty-five percent of Jesus' life, He was out of order and that He was doing what He was not called to do, and the whole congregation was getting excited and shouting amen to that! I guess Jesus must have come and visited that preacher and told him, "Hey, preacher, you know what? I made a terrible mistake, and I was wrong, so can you please let everybody know?" Seriously? Oh brother!

Yet many people feel that they cannot live by certain scriptures and, therefore, try to make the Word of God untrue! Now I can honestly say without a doubt, whom the Son sets free is *free indeed*! What is truth? "Let God be true, but every man a liar" (Roman 3:4); therefore, we know that God is truth.

The reason that people may lie is that they believe it will get them out of something, an argument, or humiliation. We lie about eating the cookie in the cookie jar; we lie about hitting Johnnie. We lie when we come home late because, after all, if we told the truth, we know that we're going hear what we don't want to hear, which is… "You are wrong!"

Who wants to be wrong when we can just lie a little lie and be right and not hear a thing about it? After all, who wants to take the blame for anything? Who wants to pay the ticket? "Uh, officer, I really didn't know the speed limit was…" "Uh, I could have sworn that the light was green when I passed it!"

When does anyone happily admit that they are wrong? "Yes, officer, I knew the speed limit was thirty-five, and I just decided to take a chance and speed, hoping not to get caught." "Yes, I saw the red light, but I am a very impatient person who has a conference to go to!" "Okay, I ate the cookie!" Can you imagine if everyone admitted to their faults? "I was late, I was inconsiderate, and yes, I should have called." "I was wrong."

Nobody wants to be responsible for their bad actions. If people actually told the truth, then maybe there would not be so many people going to divorce court or facing child custody battles. Then we wouldn't need so many juries or jury duties, and we wouldn't have to pay attorneys all those high fees simply because we were not honest with each other and because we wouldn't admit our faults and accept responsibilities. Therefore, nobody trusts anybody!

When a person lies, they are saying that they feel that their lie will make things better for them, and therefore, they are putting their trust in a lie versus putting their trust in the truth or, shall I say, in God, since He is the truth. If people came clean with each other and always told the truth, then they would be able to build their relationship on trust instead of always wondering if they were lying. And that's way better than having to continually hide so many secrets! "Shhh…don't tell mom!" Why don't you just tell the truth and get yelled at and get it over with and move on already?

The Bible says that your sins will find you out, and that means that you really can't hide anything for very long. I remember one time when I went to church with my mom, and I pulled up to the spot where the elderly and handicapped people would get dropped off because my mother was elderly. I left my car parked in that spot and took my mother inside the church.

I felt that I had the right to take my mom inside the church and everybody else just needed to wait until I was good and ready to move my car! And after all, I was a leader in the church! Bless God! I felt that since I had a lot of responsibility by taking care of my mom, I had that right to make everyone else wait! But when I saw how others were inconveniently having to go around my car, at first, I thought, *Oh, well, too bad*, but then I started to feel conviction that was setting in.

And not long after that, I got scolded by an elderly volunteer in the church who was also inconvenienced by my actions, and she scolded me but good! And when she scolded me, I was shocked that I didn't get upset with her, but instead, I humbled myself and said, "I am so sorry for being very selfish and inconsiderate." I must tell you that she was shocked when I said that! I have to say that it felt so good to tell the truth even if it was on myself!

I must admit that it's not always easy telling the truth, but I can honestly say that it is quite a relief to be truthful and admit my guilt and be able to move on. And the best thing is to have a clear conscience after I repented. When a person faces the truth and then repents and admits their faults, then their mind will get cleared up from guilt. The Bible says to "confess your faults one to another and pray for one another that ye may be healed" (James 5:16).

It's quite amazing how I can see so much more now as I read the Bible, and yes, the truth really does make a person *free*! I have been reading the Bible through for about eight years now; I honestly lost count, but I can say that my eyes have been opened wide, and what's funny is since I have been delivered from a lying spirit, I can spot a liar a mile away!

"For the Word of God is quick, and powerful, sharper than any twoedged sword, piercing even to the dividing asunder of soul and spirit, and of the joints and marrow, and is a discerner of the thoughts and intents of the heart" (Hebrews 4:12). If God's Word is in you, then you can be sure that this is pertaining to you being a discerner of thoughts and knowing the intentions of the heart.

Have you ever said, "I never saw that coming"? So now when I see a person who is trying to get close to me, I can see their intentions. Many people who are walking in darkness believe their own lie, and they will argue till they are blue in the face that what they believe is right. It's so bizarre to watch them! Sadly, there is absolutely nothing that anyone can say to a blind person that will be able to make them see, not a solitary thing!

I learned that only God can open the blind eyes. After all, it took God to open mine! So now when I look at someone who is operating in a lying spirit, I realize that they are like people who are physically blind, and no matter how much we may try to argue with someone, I know that there are no words that can change them. All we can do is pray to God that He will open their eyes so that they will be able to see the *light*.

"The king's heart is in the hand of the Lord, as the rivers of water: he turns is withersoever He will" (Proverbs 21:1). When I read this verse, I must say I got it! I got! I got it! If the king's heart is in God's hand, then our hearts are in His hand as well. So, when someone does not understand me when I try to explain something only because they are blind, then I pray to God to touch their heart. That is the key, and arguing with someone is not! Don't waste your breath, your energy, and your time trying to convince a person of what you want them to understand; instead, go to God and ask Him to touch their heart.

It's amazing what you will learn by reading God's Word. One of the scariest scriptures that I read was found in Romans 9. "Therefore hath he mercy on whom he will have mercy, and whom he will he hardeneth" (Romans 9:18). There are many examples of God hardening hearts in the Bible. One of them is Pharaoh. When God brought all those plaques to Egypt, He hardened Pharaoh's heart.

When I watched the movie *The Ten Commandments*, I always believed that Pharaoh was an idiot for not letting God's people go until I read the Bible and read that God hardened Pharaoh's heart. I don't believe that there is a human being filled with lice and boils who would refuse to let the people of God go, and those are the least of the plagues!

But the good news is that the Bible tells us that we don't have to harden our heart. "While it is said, To day if ye will hear his voice, harden not your hearts, as in the provocation" (Hebrews 3:15). When we seek God with all our heart, then He will direct our steps. "The steps of a good man are ordered by the Lord: and he delighteth in his way" (Psalm 37:23). He will guide us into all truth! Blessed be the name of the Lord!

Chapter 4

Let Patience Have Her Perfect Work

"But let patience have her perfect work, that ye may be perfect and entire, wanting nothing"

James 1:4

As my mom got older, I noticed that she was moving slower, and after a while it was a lot slower! I was always in a rush, especially when it came to going to church or taking my mom to her doctor's appointment. I was always a nervous wreck when I would get my mom ready. If you ever want to know if you need patience, then I suggest that you take care of an elderly person, and you will soon find out!

So when my mom started getting slower, I had to try and slow myself down, and that was so hard for me to do; it felt like I had to stop breathing and just die! When I tried to slow myself down, it felt like I was high on dope! (I smoked dope only a few times in my teen years, and I hated the feeling that it gave me, so I never did it again.) I'm a person who really likes to use my brain...thank you very much!

So for me to sit still and wait for my mom was very hard for me to do. At times it felt like I was like getting an electric shock treatment! What could I do...?

Absolutely nothing! I found out that *patience* really is *death*! So, when my mom started getting slower, I realized that a death process had to take place in me!

I was always used to doing things quickly, but I had no choice but to stop and take the time and wait on my mom. And each time we had to go somewhere, and I had to get her ready, I felt like I was getting a shock treatment after shock treatment, but nevertheless, I knew that I had to be patient. When God tells us to wait, words of wisdom...don't hold your breath!

So, when I tried to slow down, it literally felt like I was doing everything in slow motion, and I have to say that it felt very unnatural! However, I knew that God's Word says that we must bear fruit, and patience is one of the fruits of the Spirit. I really could not believe how impatient I was! As I stated earlier, I really thought that I was a good Christian, even a great Christian, but I was only believing a lie!

The thing is that I had absolutely no idea that I even lacked patience. I didn't realize how I acted when there was a slow-moving vehicle on the road in front of me. I always wanted to scream out, "Get off the road, you idiot!" I couldn't even see how I was acting with my mom when I would rush her to get ready. It wasn't until I started reading the Bible through that I realized a whole lot of stuff that I was doing that was not pleasing to God.

The Bible is a mirror that magnifies, and no one really wants to look at it! I know that I didn't! One of the reasons that many people don't read the Bible is that they say that they really don't have time. Yet we have the time to look at our face in the mirror and we sure spend plenty of time fixing ourselves up!

If we could only do that with our spiritual mirror...if I had only known that there was a spiritual mirror. So, when I realized how impatient I was, I knew that I had to change some way, somehow. It was not easy for me to do by no means; just put me in a coffin already! And on top of that, my mom started talking slower! "Mom, are you hungry?" "Well..."

When I started striving for patience was when I realized what it was to actually die to self. I can say that I truly learned the meaning of the death that Paul talked about. Sometimes it may feel like God will make you wait a bazillion years for something, but that all comes with the process of patience. Besides, how would we learn patience without going through the waiting process?

"And not only so, but we glory in tribulations also: knowing that tribulation worketh patience" (Romans 5:3). Nobody likes to wait, but I'm getting to the point that I have waited such a very long for God's promise that I really don't care if I get the promises or not! I just wanted God to take the pain away that I had been experiencing! Calgon!

I can honestly say that everything that I ever wanted, desired, or dreamed of having God has completely removed those desires from me. I realized that what I thought that I wanted was just my flesh craving to be noticed and for me to be famous! But when I allowed God to do the work in me, then He took His liberty!

When God started moving things out of me, then I began to have a clear vision of things that God wanted me to see. And once I began to see clearly then, I was able to see that God was everything that I really wanted and needed. The devil waits very patiently for us, and therefore, we need to be patient when we wait for God!

We really need to be patient with reading the Bible. We need to be patient with listening to God, and we need to be patient to wait for an answer from God when we ask Him for something. I must admit that there were other things that I really wanted, but I had to be so very patient, and I must say that it was not by choice, mind you, but I waited and waited and waited and waited.

I waited so much; then the craziest thing happened—the desires that I used to have just disappeared, and I actually found myself wanting…absolutely nothing! For many years, I felt like I had to have whatever I wanted, and I wanted it right now…or else! I wanted to buy that purse…and I couldn't wait for no sales either…I wanted new clothes, new jewelry, new shoes, and I wanted it *now*!

But when God gave me patience and He removed those desires from me, the great thing is that He began replacing my desires with His desires. Now I can truly say that He really is all that I want, and He's all that I need! I just can't imagine being without my God! I just can't!

I just can't imagine doing anything or going anywhere without Him coming along with me. I just can't imagine looking at the beautiful sunset without thinking about the One who created it. I just can't imagine hearing the birds singing so beautifully without knowing that my God created them to sing.

I just can't imagine hugging my dogs without imagining the One who created these furry little creatures to be such a blessing to me. I just can't imagine getting in my car and driving without asking Him to go with me to protect me. I just can't imagine eating my food without thinking of the One who created everything so perfectly in order for me to have the meals that I have: the meat, the veggies, and all the seasonings!

God not only provides food for me, but He provides great-tasting food! Even the fowls of the air know that their next meal is coming from Him. He clothes the grass of the fields, and He sends rain on the flowers…He feeds them all, and so we, being His children, really don't have to do anything but believe that if God so clothes the grass, then how much more will He clothe us?

Can you imagine if we had the responsibility of feeding all the creatures that God has created? Here, birdie birdie! If God provides food for the wild animals, and some of them are as humungous as they are, then why do we worry? Animals that live in the wild sit around and play with each other, and they don't worry about anything, yet we are human beings who want to see everything right in front of us lest we quickly panic!

We don't want to wait for anything, nor do we want to believe anything unless we see it! Our flesh wants everything now! Many times when we get what we want, we don't enjoy it for very long. We have so much, and yet we are always wanting more! Sadly, our desires blind us from seeing what we have already been given. I realize that all the stuff that I wanted was not fulfilling, nor would it have made me happy. Now I don't even want anything.

Can you imagine not wanting anything? "What would you like for your birthday?" "Nothing." Now I have to ask myself what I can do that will bring fulfillment to my life. What can I get or do that will be pleasing to me or make me happy? And surprisingly, the answer is absolutely nothing! Only God brings fulfillment to my life, and He provides everything for me so that I don't even need to desire. And if I should by chance want something like a good gluten-free pizza, He sure knows how to get me one and…He has!

Patience will come just when you can't wait anymore. Patience will kill every thought that you hoped for, and when patience comes, you will be able to trust God for everything. Not only must we wait patiently for an answer from God, but we also must be able to accept whatever answers that God gives us. When your patience is complete, it, my dear one, will honestly leave you wanting nothing.

I have to say that it really feels so good not to want anything. And if I should want something, all I have to do is ask God for it, and when I do ask for something, I don't expect it to show up at my doorstep, even though things that I have asked for have showed up at my doorstep! One time I just said out loud that I would really like to have a new set of cooking pans, and lo and behold a couple of days later, a brand-new set of pans showed up on my doorstep!

My brother, who is now with the Lord, told me that he was at a mall, and when he went to a certain store, he said that he was passing by the section with the cookware, and he said that God told him to stop and buy a set of pans for me, and of course he obeyed God; mind you, it was not a cheap set either! That's just how God works! So I don't have to sit there and ponder on what I may want or even need as I once used to, but instead, I learned to be content with what I have. "But godliness with contentment is great gain" (1 Timothy 6:6).

Now when I ask God for something, He just gives it to me because He knows that no matter what, I will be grateful with or without it. I can't tell you enough how grateful I am for the many blessings that I have now. The Bible says that if we are in Him and His Words are in us, we can ask anything, and He will do it (John 15:7). The Bible really works, y'all!

Chapter 5

What Is the Church?

Many people may think that the church is a building that Christians go to every Sunday, but as I have been seeking God, I've come to realize that the true church is not a building. The church is not a place for shouting and bucking, and it's certainly not a place where you help the preacher try to make you fall down! I used to think that the church was supposed to be a huge building that had big rallies and so-called huge revivals where people dressed up to kill in order to show everybody their fancy clothes and name tags!

There are people who think that the church is a place used to trade business cards so that other preachers can let them preach in their church so they can build a repertoire! The big question is, what happens after church when you go home to your wife, your husband, your children, and even your parents? Are people who go to church really changed? Or are they just getting pumped up for the next rally, revival, or camp meeting? What to wear? Who will be preaching and *proph-a-lying* to me tonight? Who will tell me my name and tell me where I live?

When people hear that we are Christians, what does that really mean? It used to mean something a long time ago. Now it seems like we've given Christianity a new meaning, and the new meaning says, "I'm better than you, and I should be treated with respect and given all rights to my things and yours too because I have a badge!" The new meaning also says, "I should be praised, honored, and lifted up for my talent because I am all that—

just come to the camp meetings, and you'll see...*meeeeee!*" "You'll see how important I am and how respected I am, and you will see who 'I,' 'I,' 'I,' 'I' am!"

Seems to me that when people really find out who those supposedly important people really are once exposed in the light, then those people with a big name will see and realize who they really are...*not*! Many churches today have become a laughingstock! They have also made God's Word of no effect, and not only that, but people in many churches have absolutely no effectiveness!

Years ago, my dad came to visit me and my sister Abby when we were living in California. He lived in Texas at the time. Since he was saved, he wanted to find a church for me and my sister to attend. We were not saved at the time, but my dad was ever determined to get us in a church, hoping we would get saved. So we went to this huge megachurch where thousands of people attended there. So we got a seat in the church, and we were okay with it. Then my sister and I said if someone shakes our hand in this church, then we will know that this will be our church.

So right after the service, we went to the back of the church, and the people were coming out of the church, and we were standing there waiting for someone to shake our hands. As we stood there and watched the crowds of people leaving. We kept looking for someone to say hi to us or even a "God bless you"; that would have been good enough for us. We even went as far as to hold our hands out to other people, and we would even tell them, "God bless you." And still no one stopped to say anything to us. Every single one of them went around us and just totally ignored us. Rush...rush...rush.

We waited until everybody left, and sadly, not one of them said anything to us. We had been away from church for many years already and were trying to get back in church, but after that happened, we stopped looking for a church, and we went our jolly ways. Now I don't condemn the people because I know that they are not informed by their leaders of what it is to be a real Christian. They simply don't know because they weren't taught, and that's that! "Get rich quick and be famous is our model!" Love the crowds, and well...who are the crowds, really? Does anyone really care to know?

We can see how so many people in the Middle East are getting converted to Jesus Christ left and right, and I have to say that those people who get converted are really saved people who have fallen head over heels in love with Jesus! Those people are willing to risk their lives and their family's lives to serve the God of Abraham, Isaac, and Jacob. Those people know that they are going to suffer for their faith and for their God, and they are even willing to die for Him.

There are so many people in the Middle East and in other communist countries who are facing persecution just for believing in Jesus, and others who go to those countries are being persecuted because they witness to people about Jesus. Many of those people are being tortured, starved, beaten, raped, and killed, and yet they still refuse to deny Jesus Christ. They truly understand the cross of Jesus Christ.

There are people who risk their lives just to get a Bible in someone's hands in these countries where they don't allow Bibles, and yet we Christians have several Bibles sitting around in our house and don't bother to look at them till Sunday comes around and the pastor tells us to open our Bibles! We may briefly glance through a couple of scriptures when we need something from God, yet those from other countries where it's not allowed, when they get a Bible, are clinging to every word! Sadly, sometimes, we don't even know where our Bible is!

Sometimes when I hear about people who are suffering for God, it makes me wonder if I am truly saved myself! A while back, I was watching a Christian television program, and I saw two beautiful women who were being interviewed. They were from one of those countries in the Middle East, not sure which one, and they had been locked up for their faith in Jesus. They were talking about how they were beaten and tortured in prison because of their faith, and yet when I saw them on TV, they looked so free and beautiful!

Sometimes when women go through bad things, they tend to lose their beauty, and they start looking much older, but you wouldn't even know what these women went through by looking at them. As a matter of fact, they looked like they just came from a glamorous tropical island, and they looked so beautiful and ever so refreshed! Their youth was renewed like eagles! They were so cheerful! They said that they were just happy to be able to spread the gospel to the people in prison!

Yet we sit there and whine when it's time to go to church or volunteer! We whine when we have to get up fifteen minutes early to pray and maybe get a few scriptures in our tired minds! God forbid if the pastor asks us if we have read the Bible that week! And then we sit there wondering why we get no results from our little prayer time. And we wonder why we didn't receive our healing, and we wonder why we are not blessed! We wonder why bills keep piling up, and we definitely want to know why we have no peace.

We hear about so many people who can barely get a good night's rest these days. One time when I was working on the prayer line, a woman wanted me to pray for her. She told me that the devil was messing with her sleep and that she wasn't going to allow that. I told her that if she really wanted the devil to leave her alone, she had to pick up her Bible and start reading it and the devil would put her right to sleep! As tired as she was, she cracked up so hard at that statement. Though I laughed too, yet at the same time I was thinking that really shouldn't be a reason for a person to pick up their Bible.

I remember when I used to try to read the Bible at night, I would always fall asleep. But now the first thing that I do right after I wake up, sleepy and all, is read the Bible, and when I do, I immediately feel the energy and the strength of God. I can honestly say that I have received plenty of revelation as I do, but I must admit that it took a while of reading the Bible before that happened.

When I first started reading the Bible in the morning, I would almost fall asleep, but as I kept on pursuing and reading the Bible every morning, then after a while of consistently reading is when I began to feel energized! It's kind of like working out. When you first start to work out, you won't feel one ounce of energy, but eventually, after working out for a while, you will.

Do people read the Bible because they consider it a chore? It wasn't till I faced this trial that I wanted answers from God. And that was when I got alone with God and began to search His Word as He instructed me to. It was sad that it took going through a trial for me to seek Him. God simply wanted a relationship with me.

Sadly, many people who have a relationship with God start out good in the beginning, but after a while they end up like so many marriages today. We can see so many times that after couples have been married for a while, they start getting quiet, they stop talking and become distant, and then they simply don't even notice that their spouse is even there. Then after a while, they start to wish that they weren't there! And so goes it with God.

It seems like when we first get saved, we love on God, but as time goes by, we stop talking to Him, and then after a while, we simply don't notice Him. What a dull and boring Christian life that is! At least these two women who were locked up in prison and beaten had some excitement about reaching the lost! They said they went to preach to the prostitutes in the prisons and were getting souls saved! They were excited about getting the prisoners set free from the bondages of sin! Now that's exciting! These women knew that they didn't have anything to lose because they had already lost everything for the gospel of Jesus Christ.

There are many Christians today who don't have an ounce of joy, and many of them don't even know the meaning of peace. Many Christians who try to witness to others don't even have a clue about who God really is, and that's simply because they haven't studied God's Word. We must realize that the Word really is God. "In the beginning was the Word, and the Word was with God, and the Word was God" (John 1:1).

People may try to witness about what they have experienced, but that's all they have to talk about because they have no knowledge about the God they say that they are serving! God is so much more than a miracle or an experience, and yet sadly, many Christians today don't know Him; they just know about a building called the church.

Many people just know what someone told them about God or what they heard the preacher preach about God. In order for us to be the church, we must know what the Bible says about being the church. The Bible tells us that our bodies are the temple of God and that His Spirit dwells in us (1 Corinthians 3:16). When Jesus came on this earth, He called twelve disciples. He didn't tell them to open a church building and make it big; instead, He showed them how to be the church.

The Bible says, "The kingdom of God is within [us]" (Luke 17:21). God called His people to bear fruit, and He calls those who bear fruit His disciples. "Herein is my Father glorified, that ye bear much fruit; so shall ye be my disciples" (John 15:8). Also, John 15 talks about those who don't bear fruit.

Jesus told His disciples to go and preach.

And he said unto them, "Go ye into all the world, and preach the gospel to every creature. He that believeth and is baptized shall be saved; but he that believeth not shall be damned.

And these signs shall follow them that believe; In my name shall they cast out devils; they shall speak with new tongues; They shall take up serpents; and if they drink any deadly thing, it shall not hurt them; they shall lay hands on the sick, and they shall recover. So then after the Lord had spoken unto them, He was received up into heaven, and sat on the right hand of God. And they went forth, and preached everywhere, the Lord working with them, and confirming the word with signs following. Amen."

Mark 16:15–20

Jesus told them to go in all the world, and verse 20 says that they went and preached everywhere, and as they did, then the Lord worked with them and confirmed His Word with signs following. This is what many Christians lack today. Why? Because people are trying to make the church building the church instead of becoming the church. We are to be a witness wherever we go. As a church, we are to be salt and light wherever we go. "Let your light so shine before men, that they may see your good works, and glorify your Father which is in heaven" (Matthew 5:16).

People are looking for something different. So many people are just tired of going to church because they don't see any kind of light or salt from Christians who are supposed to bear fruit, and that's why so many people are leaving so many churches. That's the reason so many churches have shut down.

If people want to experience the true church instead of just attending a building and saying that the building is the church, then they need to seek God's Word and let God mold them and shape them into what He intended for the church to be like. Do people even know that they are God's temple? "Know ye not that ye are the temple of God, and that the Spirit of God dwelleth in you?" (1 Corinthians 3:16). "What? know ye not that your body is the temple of the Holy Ghost which is in you, which ye have of God, and ye are not your own? We are the Temple of the Living God" (1 Corinthians 6:19).

We as Christians should represent God wherever we go, and not just in church. People today see nothing but darkness as the world goes...we should be shining lights...this little light of mine...I'm gonna let it shine, let it shine, let it shine, let it shine! I must say that it took me a long time for my light to really shine. I remember one time I went to get some food from I believe it was Burger King. I went to the drive-through.

When I placed my order, I must say that I was not really acting like a Christian because when I was telling the guy my order, I was demanding and commanding him how to make my French fries hot and my burger right! So, when I went to the window to pay, lo and behold, the person who took my order was a church member! Talk about feeling low! I felt like an idiot! And at that time, I was a leader in the church!

There was another time that I had gone to the grocery store. It was very cold outside, and I hate cold weather! I had my mom's handicap sticker hanging on my car mirror. So I took my liberty, and I parked in a handicapped spot. So I got out of the car and started walking to the store, and all of a sudden, I heard a lady screaming.

There was a gentleman standing outside of the grocery store who was an usher at the church, and we started talking and walking inside the store and this lady started yelling louder. I didn't know what she was screaming about. So the usher told me that she was screaming at me! So I walked up to her and asked what she wanted. She started yelling at me for parking at a handicapped parking spot.

She told me that I didn't look handicapped, and she demanded that I move my car. I tried to explain how I had problems with my back, which at that time I did, but she didn't care; she kept saying that I didn't look handicapped. So I just said, "Yes, ma'am!" and I moved my car from that handicapped spot. Boy, was I ever humiliated once again! I have to say that there was no shine in my light!

A few years ago, I was looking in this Christian magazine that sold Christian items such as Bibles, Christian CDs and T-shirts with Christian logos, and things like that. I saw some nice caps with Christian logos on them that I really liked, and so I ordered several of them. This was years later after I had my encounter with God.

I like wearing caps, and so I started wearing them, but I realized that my light was still dim. I still had an attitude! I would get upset a lot, and I knew that I was not representing God like I should. So I had to stop wearing my caps because I did not want to misrepresent God. I knew that there was still work that needed to be done in me.

I can humbly say that it took some time for God to work on my attitude, and now I can wear my caps! I must admit that sometimes I still mess up, and my caps remind me that I am representing God! I never want to be a Christian who turns people off to God when they see my actions.

I'm not saying by any means for people not to attend church; we know that the churches were established in the Bible. What I am saying is that when people attend a church, they should be able to experience other Christian people who are full of the fruit of the Spirit of God and who have the love, joy, compassion, and the peace of God flowing through them.

The Bible says the Lord added to the church daily. People should attend church so that they can grow in the faith, get encouraged, and have fellowship with one another. Sadly, not too many churches experience that. There are so many lonely people who go to church who just want someone to talk to and greet them with a smile.

I used to always get to church early so that I could get a front-row seat. I wanted to be as close to the front as I possibly could be. I felt like if I was in the front row, I would get more blessed. I was a leader of my church, and I would meet and greet the congregation, and mind you, I was good at it! I didn't realize that I wanted to be noticed and I wanted to be seen. I thought that I was all that until I began to look in the mirror of the Word of God!

The crazy thing is that people thought that I was all that too! People in the church looked up to me, and they would always compliment me. There were leaders in my church who hated me and didn't want me to sit in the front-row seats, and they fought me tooth and nail! Of course, I fought them back, and I have to say that I won! I won, and they couldn't do anything about it! This was the church! Leaders fighting leaders for a seat! One of the leaders made my elderly mom move from our seat while I was greeting people, and when I told her something, she got so mad that she actually wanted to take me outside and fight me!

After a while, things got rough where I was living. There were a lot of bad things that started happening in my neighborhood. Sex offenders started moving in, and houses were being robbed left and right. They were stealing cars and spray-painting people's garages. I took it as a sign to get out of there! They would send us pictures of the sex offenders who moved in my neighborhood, and then I saw one standing outside of my house with a big smile! That was it!

So I told my mom that we needed to move. So we moved to another state for a while, and then we moved to Texas. I had not been to church for a few years. I had attended other churches between states, and I really didn't know what to expect at these churches. I felt that there should be a move of the Holy Spirit in the churches that I had attended, but there was not much of that. I wanted to feel something; I wanted to see a move of God. I wanted to hear anointed preachers scream and shout the house down!

I can say that despite all the wonderful things that I had experienced with God while seeking Him in my alone time with Him, I was still lost! I guess I was still looking for a move of God from or through men! I realized that I was looking for what I experienced in big churches, rallies, camp meetings, etc.

I was taught how to be a Christian, and I was also taught how to do things the way Christian people did things. It was instilled in me, and it needed to come out of me. Since I have been reading the Bible through, I know what the preacher is preaching only because I have been reading the Bible through for years. I know that I should be attending a church, but because I am not learning anything new, I feel like I'm not getting anything out of being at a church.

Am I supposed to be the one who shouts amen? And who yells, "Preach, preacher!"? I have to say that is not fulfilling at all, and I end up feeling like… um…dry, and I feel like I have accomplished nothing by that. Am I supposed to just show up and sit in the pew and make the pastor happy as I root him on and then go home? Please tell me that there is more to this church thing! The good news is that God showed me that there is!

This is not how church is supposed to be. Preachers preach a good sermon then they give an altar call for people to get saved, and then they tell people to come to church and get involved. Okay, I did all that! My question is, what happened to God? The last time that I went to church, I got a good seat in the front row, and I enjoyed the preaching, but I already knew the things that the preacher preached, and at the end of the service, everyone walked out. It was over! So what did I gain from going?

I would wake up early to do this; mind you, I am not a morning person! I can't believe that I attended church for so many years and ended up going home feeling empty. A few years ago, I worked for a church. I had to work on Sundays, and I was not happy about that because I wanted to be in church! I was able to watch a little bit of service on the computer on my break, but not much.

I wanted to jump, sing, shout, and dance! But then my job ended, and I was able to attend church for a while, but then Covid-19 hit, and everything closed down, and frankly, so did I! But when I was finally able to attend church, then I realized something. I realized that I am not there for myself, but I am supposed to be there for others.

I am not supposed to be sitting in the front row, but my job is to be there to minister to the people in the church. I don't mean that I'm supposed to be a minister in the church, but as a Christian, I'm supposed to be a light shining so that others around me can see my light shining and be encouraged and strengthened. I've gone to church long enough for myself, and now it's time for me to go to church to be a blessing to other people in the church!

The front-row seats should really be for the newcomers; they should feel welcomed as they walk in the doors of the church. Newcomers should by no means have to fight for a good seat, but instead they should feel like they came to the right place! Jesus came to serve! It's so sad that servanthood is not in a lot of church categories! Any Christian who has unsaved family members would feel so happy if their lost loved one went to church and got to sit in a front-row seat! I know that I would feel that way about my unsaved loved ones.

We really should feel the same way for anyone who is lost and not just our loved ones. When a person comes to church and gives their life to God, the Bible says that the angels rejoice over one person who repents! "Likewise, I say unto you, there is joy in the presence of the angels of God over one sinner that repenteth" (Luke 15:10).

The Bible says that God is no respecter of persons, and neither should we be! One thing that I can honestly say is that God has totally delivered me from thinking highly of anyone. I have been set free from that! I really don't care how many degrees someone has or how talented they are. I don't even care how anointed they are. I don't praise anyone!

People are people, and everyone makes mistakes! Just look at King Solomon, the wisest man in the world, next to Jesus. King Solomon had all that wisdom, and he was unhappy, and not only that, with all that he knew, he messed up terribly! I've learned that absolutely no one is perfect! God is a jealous God, and He made it very clear to me that He *alone* wants to be worshipped!

"For thou shalt worship no other god: for the Lord, whose name is Jealous, is a jealous God" (Exodus 34:14). "For the Lord thy God is a consuming fire, even a jealous God" (Deuteronomy 4:24). "God is jealous, and the Lord revengeth; the Lord revengeth, and is furious; the Lord will take vengeance on his adversaries, and he reserveth wrath for his enemies" (Nahum 1:2).

I admit that I had been worshipping people! I was in awe of anyone who had a big title, spoke smoothly and wore an expensive suit, and had an anointing that followed! I was ever impressed! Until I began to see how God brought down many preachers, evangelists, and so forth who were lifted way up! To me, that was a big shocker! The real shocker was that God used these people in a mighty way, and then they fell! They were indeed anointed! But God let me know that people, including myself, were making idols of people like that, and He didn't like it one bit!

People in the church need to know that they are not beneath the leaders. They must respect authority and submit to authority because God commands it, but not because they think so highly of them. They must remember that God has given everyone a job, and that is to serve others. Can you imagine a church like that? To me, it's sad when I hear the words, "God is going to use you greatly! You are going to be great! You have a great calling on your life!" Though that may be such a rush for people to hear, I just have to say, get over it! Get over yourself! Seriously?

God is the Only Great One, and everyone else is a servant of God! "But if ye have respect to persons, ye commit sin, and are convinced of the law as transgressors" (James 2:9).

> *At the same time came the disciples unto Jesus, saying, Who is the greatest in the kingdom of heaven? And Jesus called a little child unto him, and set him in the midst of them, And said, Verily I say unto you, Except ye be converted, and become as little children, ye shall not enter into the kingdom of heaven.*
>
> *Whosoever therefore shall humble himself as this little child, the same is greatest in the kingdom of heaven.*
>
> Matthew 18:1–4

"So, the last shall be first, and the first last: for many be called, but few chosen" (Matthew 20:16). "And He said unto them, Whosoever shall receive this child in my name receiveth me: and whosoever shall receive me receiveth him that sent me: for he that is least among you all, the same shall be great" (Luke 9:48). Many churches have it backward!

A pastor's job is to get their congregations close to God so that they can be led by God and not by man. If a person wants to know who God really is, they need to know His Word because, once again, the Word is Him. It's not good enough for the people to get the revelation of some preacher, but they need to get their own revelation of the God that they are serving so that God Himself can direct them where He wants them to go and to do what He wants them to do and to be what God wants them to be.

But in order for people to be the church, they need to know the God that they are serving is very real in their lives. And when people actually get to know the God of the Bible, then they can be sure that God will direct their steps and lead them in the path that they should go. God is all about saving people from destruction and bringing them into His marvelous light.

God wants His church together, and He wants them to be one because when we are one, then nobody can get left out. I would encourage everyone to read John 17 and its totality. This is what Jesus prayed before He was persecuted. This is His desire for the church. "And this is life eternal, that they might know thee the only true God, and Jesus Christ, whom thou hast sent" (John 17:3). "That they all may be one; as thou, Father, art in me, and I in thee, that they also may be one in us: that the world may believe that thou hast sent me" (John 17:21).

Chapter 6

Sons and Daughters of God

When God created this world and everything in it, it was totally perfect! He created the man and the woman perfectly. They had no imperfections whatsoever, and they were meant to live forever and ever and ever in the beautiful garden of Eden. They did not get old, and neither did their bodies. Unfortunately, things got all messed up!

Adam and Eve decided to do what God told them not to do, and they ate the forbidden fruit. When that happened, then sadly because of their one mistake, the world was turned completely upside down! Why couldn't they just obey one commandment? Why? God created man and woman so that He could commune with them, but we know the story of how Satan deceived Eve, and she listened to him way too many times until she actually believed what he said.

When Satan talked to Eve, he used the very words of God to deceive her, and sadly it worked! When that happened, God had to remove them out of that beautiful garden that He created for them to enjoy because of their disobedience. They had to leave the garden because God also had placed a tree of life in the garden, and if they had eaten it, then they would have lived forever and ever in their sinful state and never be able to die (Genesis 2:9). Now that's a scary thought!

When they disobeyed God, then all mankind became infected with sin, and both men and women had to live a hard life. Men have to labor, and women have labor, giving birth! Before the fall, Adam and Eve didn't know sin, nor did they know what evil was, but now, through their disobedience, all mankind is born in sin, and sadly, we were all born cursed! We were all born evil, and we were all born dumb!

If you read through the Bible, you will see just how mixed up the people were! God chose Israel to be His people, and yet they still did really bad things against Him. When I first began reading through the Bible, it was quite mind-boggling, but once I continued reading through year after year, and then the Holy Spirit helped me understand it more clearly.

At first, I thought that the people were just so dumb for not obeying God, especially because God would bless them when they obeyed Him, but as I kept reading through, I realized that we all became really dumb when Adam and Eve disobeyed God. When Adam and Eve disobeyed God, then our flesh took dominance over the spirit, and we know that our flesh just wants to do whatever it doggone pleases!

When sin entered in man, then man then became vile, vicious, cunning, lustful, hateful, prideful, egotistic, fearful, liars...and the list goes on and on; just think of your ex-boyfriend, girlfriend, husband, or wife, and you can fill in whatever else that you want! The reasons your exes are the way they are is simply because they were all born that way!

That's the reason God sent the flood to destroy all the people in the world, except for Noah and his family, and when I read about that, I saw how that didn't even work. I thank God that He had a plan! He had a master plan indeed! "For the Son of man is come to seek and to save that which was lost" (Luke 19:10). He had to pay a high price; we all know that He had to die a most horrible and shameful death on the cross so that we could be free from sin.

For God so loved the world so much, and that's why He sent His only Son, Jesus, to die on the cross. God's purpose was to get back that communion with man that He once had with Adam and Eve. The reason that He came was so that He could make us His sons and daughters, but in order for Him to do that, He had to go through a process of denying Himself.

Jesus had to kill His flesh. He literally had to carry His cross to His death, and the Bible tells us that we must do the same.

Saying, The Son of man must suffer many things, and be rejected of the elders and chief priests and scribes, and be slain, and be raised the third day. And he said to them all, If any man will come after me, let him deny himself, and take up his cross daily, and follow me.

For whosoever will save his life shall lose it: but whosoever will lose his life for my sake, the same shall save it.

Luke 9:22–24

The Bible says, "As many as received Him, to them gave He power to become the sons of God even to them that believe on His Name" (John 1:12). It also says, "For as many as are led by the Spirit of God, they are the sons of God" (Romans 8:14).

We don't hear many preachers who teach their congregations to be led by the Spirit of God. This is why it is so essential to read the Bible. "My people are destroyed for lack of knowledge: because thou hast rejected knowledge, I will also reject thee, that thou shalt be no priest to me: seeing thou hast forgotten the law of thy God, I will also forget thy children" (Hosea 4:6).

If people just go to church on Sundays and Wednesdays to hear their pastor preach, then what they preach or teach is all they are going to know and nothing more unless they spend time in the Word. And if we can be real, how much of the preaching or teaching do we really remember once we leave the church? "How was church?" "It was great!" "What did the preacher preach about?" "Uhm."

God wanted to get me on my own so He could be my teacher. "It is written in the prophets, and they shall be all taught of God. Every man therefore that had heard, and hath learned of the Father, cometh unto me" (John 6:45). "But the anointing which ye have received of Him abideth in you and ye need not that any man teach you: but the same anointing teaches you all things, and is truth, and is no lie, and even as it has taught you, ye shall abide in Him" (1 John 2:27).

Many people attend church just to get a quick fix as I did. I remember one time when I went to church, I actually told one of the elders of the church that I needed my fix, and I actually rolled up my sleeve like a junkie! We both laughed about it, but the sad truth is that I really was a junkie for someone else's anointing! I could not miss one service, and if I did, I would feel like I was going through withdrawals! Many people today are addicted to famous preachers!

When I first started going through my trial, I was devastated, and that was when I went to God and cried my head off! I was screaming and shouting at God, telling Him that I wanted some answers! God let me scream, holler, shout, go ballistic, and yell from the top of my lungs until I couldn't anymore! And that was the beginning of my journey with my King Jesus!

After God had told me to read the Bible, I began reading it, and then I began to see the real me, not the Christian me! And when I saw who I really was, I got so sick because I saw how disgusting I was! So, during my prayer time, I could not speak, but I just lay on the floor. I couldn't move. I literally felt like I was lying in my vomit! I believe I was loathing myself!

I did this for days because that was all I could do! I saw my inward parts! I saw my heart! I saw my withering, rotten, smelly, disgusting fruits! But thank God that He didn't leave me there! But little by little, I began to bathe in His Word and get cleansed from all that filth! God began cleansing me from all unrighteousness! He is faithful, and He is just!

When I saw myself was when I realized that I was so busy chasing preachers instead of chasing God! As I said before, I used to look at preachers as though they were really great! I magnified them! But as I watched many of them fall one by one, it hit me like a bombshell, and I went into utter shock! I believe the main reason for me going into shock was that I felt like my soul was in these preachers' hands, and I felt like they were responsible for where my soul would end up. I'm telling you that I was in total shock!

I watched preachers fall one by one. They had many followers who would follow them wherever they went just to be in their service. I believe that because of that, so many people were disappointed when they fell, and they may have lost their way because of it. The Bible says, "Because iniquity shall abound, the love of many shall wax cold" (Matthew 24:12).

I would hear so many preachers preaching on prosperity messages and "getting rich quick" sermons: "Just give your money and keep looking in the mailbox!" But I rarely heard anyone talking about denying self. The reason that no one wants to talk about denying self and crucifixion is because they know that no one wants to hear that kind of message. I have been going through nothing but crucifixion since God got my attention, and it actually feels like I am being self-destructive!

I have been totally ignoring my desires. Once again, it wasn't by choice. I realized that selfishness was the thing that was actually killing me! The Bible says that we are to not love the world neither the things in it...or else the love of the Father is not in us (1 John 2:15). Little by little, everything was being stripped from me, and I must stress that I didn't give up anything of myself, nor would I have, but I had to let go of a lot of things because of my circumstances. I'm just being real!

When my mom got very sick, I had to give up everything so that I could take care of her. I had to stop thinking about what I wanted or wanted to do for that matter. The crazy thing is that when I first started going to church, I really never wanted to do much of anything in my life but to praise God. Believe it or not, that was my only fun! That was my joy! That was what I lived for and loved to do! That was my passion! But as I continued going to church then that slowly faded away.

I would still do those things, but I was unknowingly doing it in the flesh and not in the Spirit. And because of my circumstances, even that had to stop, and I was upset about that! I went through withdraws! At first, I tried to blame the devil for what was happening to me until I realized that God was in total control of my life. I realized that whatever was happening to me, God was allowing it.

I can see that He has allowed everything to happen for a reason. I was going through a crisis in my life! I was going through a crucifixion! And even as I am writing, I am going through a death. I realize that death is an ongoing thing! If the apostle Paul, who wrote two-thirds of the New Testament, said that he had to die daily, then we certainly can't expect to be exempted (1 Corinthians 15:31).

Jesus also had to learn obedience through His sufferings, and if Jesus had to learn it that way, then we must too. "Though he were a Son, yet learned he obedience by the things which he suffered" (Hebrews 5:8). I so thank God that He was merciful enough to shorten the days of our lives here on this planet so that we might have hope to continue to go on with our short days and be able to bear this thing called life! Can you imagine living on this planet for nine hundred years?

The Bible says that God came to give us life more abundantly, and yet I seemed to always find myself miserably dying! I realized that death is the way to life. We must die to ourselves so that Christ can reside in us and completely take over! As we decrease, He increases! "Always bearing about in the body the dying of the Lord Jesus, that the life also of Jesus might be made manifest in our body. For we which live are always delivered unto death for Jesus' sake, that the life also of Jesus might be made manifest in our mortal flesh" (2 Corinthians 4:10–11).

Luke chapter 8 talks about the sower sowing seed that brings forth fruit. The seed is the Word of God. So then if we are reading the Bible, then we can expect growth, but if we are not, then we really can't expect anything! No more than we can expect anything to grow in the ground if we don't plant any seed.

> *Now the parable is this: The seed is the word of God. Those by the way side are they that hear; then cometh the devil, and taketh away the word out of their hearts, lest they should believe and be saved. They on the rock are they, which, when they hear, receive the word with joy; and these have no root, which for a while believe, and in time of temptation fall away.*
>
> *And that which fell among thorns are they, which, when they have heard, go forth, and are choked with cares and riches and pleasures of this life, and bring no fruit to perfection. But that on the good ground are they, which in an honest and good heart, having heard the word, keep it, and bring forth fruit with patience.*
>
> Luke 8:11–15

"And other fell on good ground, and sprang up, and bare fruit an hundredfold. And when he had said these things, he cried, He that hath ears to hear, let him hear" (Luke 8:8).

You can keep looking for tomatoes to grow. I mean, you can keep looking just like most Christians do, hoping something will be there, hoping to change without planting God's Word, but I can assure that you won't find anything! "So then faith cometh by hearing, and hearing by the word of God" (Romans 10:17).

When I was going through this trial, I stated that I wanted to get drunk, and that was simply because I had no faith that God was with me, nor did I know who God was. I was not reading my Bible, and you could say that I kept believing for tomatoes to grow! Sadly, I came to find out that I had absolutely no fruit whatsoever! I was as fruitless as they come! I was just an imitation Christian! I was a wannabe! I was Stepford's wife! I was clean on the outside but filthy on the inside! I was living in utter darkness, and I didn't even know it!

So I yelled, and I screamed at God, and I told Him that if He was there, then He'd better make Himself known, and to my surprise, He did just that! As I have been going through a death, I must say that there are times that I literally feel like I am being strangled to death! But through all that I had suffered and continued to suffer, I can honestly say that I was starting to feel better about suffering when I realized that suffering is in order.

When people hear preachers preaching on worshipping in Spirit and in truth, they really don't comprehend the true meaning. Even though some people may feel God's presence during the worship services, they may feel like they are worshipping God in the Spirit as I have always thought I was until I began searching the Bible.

The Bible says that we must live after the Spirit so that we can have life and peace (Romans 8:6). Even though there have been many times that I would feel the overwhelming presence of God in a church service, and I can tell you that His presence was very real, even when I had felt His awesome presence time and time again, I still didn't find myself having that peace that the scripture talks about.

Galatians 5 talks about the fruit of the Spirit that we are to live by; I talk about that later in this book. It's one thing for us to feel God's presence when we are around someone who is anointed, but it's altogether different when we are alone with God and feel His awesome presence abiding inside of us!

When I first began reading the Bible through, let me tell you that I was in utter shock when I read how the Bible talks a lot on a death, crucifixion, and denying self! That basically means that we must die to our desires, wants, dreams, and even our way of thinking. I learned that we must do that so that God can give us His desires, wants, dreams, and way of thinking. Is it easy? Not one bit! But neither is working out or starting a business or going to college or playing in the Olympics, and the list goes on, being married and having children. Everything that I mentioned consists of denying self if a person truly wants to succeed.

God only wants us to deny the bad things in us so He can replace them with good things. Just as an overweight person wants to shed those pounds, we, too, must shed our ungodly ways. The great news is that God will do the work when we yield our lives over to Him. Once the seed of the Word of God is planted, then we can be assured that it will grow!

When we are planting God's Word in us, we are actually planting God in us. The more Word we plant, the more God we plant, and the less Word we plant, well, don't expect too many tomatoes to grow! Since faith comes by hearing the Word of God, when we read His Word, then faith will come, and it will help us to believe what we are reading. When we start believing His Word, then we can just relax and let God continue to do His Work in us.

The Bible says that it is "He [God] which hath begun a good work in you will perform it till the day of Jesus Christ" (Philippians 1:6). "For it is God which worketh in you both to will and to do of his good pleasure" (Philippians 2:13). I take that as face value. I know now that I cannot change myself. I tried to change myself to be the person who I thought that I should be, but it was all an act!

I simply learned how to be the perfect Christian that I thought that I should be by watching other Christians who I felt were perfect, but I was just acting the part! I would say the right things with my mouth, but my heart was not in it. People who try to act like a Christian without going through the death part are just going through the motions. I can say that there is absolutely no satisfaction in that.

The Bible says that we are saved by grace through faith and not of works lest we ourselves should boast, which means getting big-headed! (Ephesians

2:8). I realize that when I am sleeping, it gives my flesh time to arise because my flesh is tired, and when I'm tired, I really don't have strength to fight. So, when I wake up feeling tired and cranky, I know that's when I need to start crucifying my flesh!

We may not realize it, but I'm finding out that when we are tired, the enemy tries his best to creep in and make us stumble. I thank God that even when I am tired, the spirit is still willing! "Watch and pray, that ye enter not into temptation: the spirit indeed is willing, but the flesh is weak" (Matthew 26:41).

So once I'm done crucifying this ugly thing that I call a blob, then God's Holy Spirit begins to take over. It's just like when you first wake up and look in the mirror. You look at your messy hair and see the crust in your eyeballs. You don't want to go outside looking like that! Well, the same applies to our spirit man.

When I first wake up, I get my coffee, and then I immediately I get in my Word; forget about looking in the mirror at my face! So instead of seeing my ugly face first thing in the morning, I look at my ugly flesh, and I can see that it needs a good wash! We still live in a body that wants and wants and wants and…and we still live in a body that reacts if it does not get what it wants!

Before Saul became the apostle Paul, he was in a very high position. We know that people in high positions, if they are not on guard, can get quite arrogant. And even when God changed his name from Saul to Paul, we can see that he still had to fight an ongoing fight of faith! Every day, I pray for God to help my doubt and unbelief.

When I'm really tired, I notice that those thoughts of fear and worries will immediately start attacking my mind. I hate those thoughts, but that was my mind that was talking to me! Now, I can honestly say that I don't get those thoughts like I used to, and I sleep like a baby. The Bible says that we have the mind of Christ. When I can have Jesus Christ's mind, then why in the world would I want my own stinking mind?

When God says that He gave us the power to become His sons and daughters, that means that He gave us power. He gave us His power to change, which means that we should be able to think, act, and live like Jesus lived. Jesus was a prime example of how we should be. He didn't give us

His commandments and just tell us to obey them like He did in the Old Testament, but instead He gave us the power to obey them.

He also gave us His Holy Spirit to guide us and to help us change so that we can become His sons and daughters. Every day, when I wake up, I can say that I feel that something in my life has changed. I compare it to watching flowers that begin to grow; little by little, they come out until they are fully blossomed. The only difference is that the flowers eventually die, but if we continue to plant His Word in our lives on a daily basis, then we can expect our fruit to grow and to increase.

"My little children, these things write I unto you, that ye sin not. And if any man sin, we have an advocate with the Father, Jesus Christ the righteous" (1 John 2:1). We see that the Bible is referring to little children. When a person comes to God, He or she is like a newborn child, and we know that children need to be nourished, fed, and trained into becoming adults.

Even though I had been a Christian for many years and was even given part as a leader, because I did not know God's Word, then I was still a child in Christ. Have you ever known someone who is a full-grown adult and yet they still act just like a child? I'm sure that we may have all come across someone like that. To me it's quite shocking to watch, but nevertheless, some people just don't grow up!

The Bible says, "For as many as are led by the Spirit of God, they are the sons of God" (Romans 8:14). Verse 19 says that we are waiting for the manifestations of sons and daughters, and verse 23 says that we are "waiting for the adoption to wit." When I started reading the Bible through, I noticed a change in my life. When I realized how badly off I was living because I did not know the Bible, nor was I living according to it, I desperately wanted to change. I just didn't know how to, but thank God He knew!

Once I started reading God's Word, then God taught me everything that I needed to know in order for me to change and for me to continue to grow. I must say that I was taking baby steps at first, and the great thing is when I fell, I would cry out to God, and He would be right there to pick me up! God is merciful and full of compassion.

God is doing the work in us. We are His workmanship created unto good works, but we must do our part by seeking Him and yielding ourselves over to Him. Growing up is not easy! People who come to Christ want to live for God, but they really don't know where to start. I thought I did! I heard the dos and the don'ts all my life, but I was never taught the "how to" part until I finally met my personal Savior.

I knew of Him, and I knew that He was real through experiencing His divine presence, but I did not know Him personally. Many preachers tell their congregation what they think about God, and they really do not know God at all. That's because they don't know their Bible. So, once again, I yelled at God, and I told Him that I wanted to be led by the Spirit and that I wanted to be His daughter, and immediately after I said that, I felt something; it was like my belly leaped! I knew that I had tapped into the spiritual realm, and that was when my journey with God began!

There are Christians who believe that they cannot change the way they are. They will use God's grace so they can continue living the same way that they have been living. They feel that they are okay with that; after all, the preachers don't tell them any different! So they continue living a life of greasy grace!

"For there are certain men crept in unawares, who were before of old ordained to this condemnation, ungodly men, turning the grace of our God into lasciviousness, and denying the only Lord God, and our Lord Jesus Christ" (Jude 1:4).

Then there are Christians who have witnessed many miracles that they know that only God could do. They may have witnessed a person being healed from an incurable disease or heard about an addict who has totally been delivered from an addiction, but when it comes down to believing that God can change them or deliver them from sin, then you will hear people beginning to doubt that God can do that.

Many Christians will easily believe the scripture that by Jesus' stripes we are healed and really believe that God will heal them, but when it comes to changing them on the inside, then we hear the words, "Don't judge me!" or "That's the way that I was born!" I have even heard some people say, "God made me this way!" Then there are those who say, "We all got our demons!" Just how sad is that?

I most certainly am not claiming no demons to be mine! And if I should find out that I have some demons, you better believe that I am going to get to casting them out and quick! I can do that because God's Word says that greater is He that is in me than he that is in the world! (1 John 4:4). God is way greater than any *impy* demon! God is soooooo great, and absolutely nothing is impossible with Him! The problem is that many Christians don't believe this. We must remember that God acts on faith.

The Bible tells us that we have all been given a measure of faith. That measure of faith was given for us to accept Christ into our hearts and to believe that Jesus was born of a virgin and died on a cross for our sins. But in order for our faith to increase, we must read God's Word. As I stated, I didn't feel like I had any faith. I thank God that He dealt me a measure of faith so that I could go to Him with my problems with my little faith!

"If we confess our sins, he is faithful and just to forgive us our sins, and to cleanse us from all unrighteousness" (1 John 1:9); that means *all* unrighteousness! Now people may not want to hear this simply because they don't really believe it can happen, but to me, this verse is so precious! All we have to do is confess our sins and sincerely mean it, and God will do all the cleansing! How wonderful is that! God is doing the work!

I remember how I used to get down on myself all the time when I would sin! I wanted to die because I felt like I had completely let God down, and I felt so undeserving! There were times that I wouldn't even look up at God because of a sin that I committed. I didn't sin a lot because God really delivered me from many of my sins.

It wasn't till recently that I realized that God is doing the work in me. Even though I have read the Bible many times over, it just hit me now. Now if I should sin, I tell God to carve away! He's the potter! We simply must believe that He is the potter and allow Him to continue His work as we continue to seek Him.

Jesus is the Word manifested! (John 1:14). The Bible says:

> *That which was from the beginning, which we have heard, which we have seen with our eyes, which we have looked upon, and our hands have handled, of the Word of life; (For the life was manifested, and we have seen it, and bear witness, and shew unto you that eternal life, which was with the Father, and was manifested unto us).*
>
> 1 John 1:1–2

"For there are three that bear record in heaven, the Father, the Word, and the Holy Ghost: and these three are one" (1 John 5:7).

For someone to really believe in God, they must believe in His Word. I know that I am repeating that God is the Word many times, and that's because it is so vital for you to really get this. If you are really serious about knowing God and about having close relationship with Him and about changing, this is the key. "It is written, Man shall not live by bread alone, but by EVERY WORD that proceedeth out of the mouth of God" (Matthew 4:4).

Sadly, so many preachers only want to preach the part of the Bible that tickles people's ears. There are many people who say that anything else outside of what they preach is just being religious. I will say that my ears have been tickled by many preachers, but come morning time, I can say that I never woke up laughing!

I had a sure 'nuff good time laughing during service because the anointing was so great, and I had a sure 'nuff good time dancing my dance and shouting my shout, but in the morning time, I was hanging my head in sadness and feeling empty. After many years of reading God's Word and in prayer and fasting, I feel like I'm going through the process of growing up from a child and becoming a mature daughter of God.

I feel like a heavy load has been lifted off me. I can say that I'm not quite where I want to be, but I believe that soon I will be. I can also say that I'm not where I used to be, but I can honestly say that I've come a long way! Too often people want to call Christians who actually live a righteous life and call them self-righteous because they don't wallow in sin, or shall I say they have been set free from sin.

> *Whosoever believeth that Jesus is the Christ is born of God: and every one that loveth him that begat loveth him also that is begotten of him. By this we know that we love the children of God, when we love God, and keep his commandments. For this is the love of God, that we keep his commandments: and his commandments are not grievous.*
>
> 1 John 5:1–3

Sadly, many people can't seem to believe that God dwells in Christians who live a sanctified life. They don't believe that God is working through them. They refuse to believe that a person can live after the Spirit and not after the flesh and actually bear good fruit. But I'm here to tell you that one day I looked in the mirror, and I didn't like what I saw. I called myself a Christian because I was doing all the things that Christians did, but when I took a good look in the mirror of the Word of God…I *saw the light*! I once was blind, but now…I *see*!

Right now, I can tell you that I cannot do what Jesus did, nor can I do greater works than He did as the Bible says that we can do. I don't doubt what it says that I can do, but the only reason that I would want to do greater works is so that God will be glorified and for people to come to God. I really cringe at the thought of having a big name for myself!

I can say that now that I'm getting to know my God more each day, I really don't have the desire to even do great works, but my desire is to know my Jesus more and have a greater relationship with Him and to make Him proud of me by letting my light shine and being a witness for Him.

When Jesus gave His disciples the authority to pray for the sick and cast out devils, they went and did exactly that. When they came back, they were so excited and full of joy telling Jesus how the devils were subject to them, but Jesus told them that was not what they needed to be excited about; what they really needed to be excited about was that their names were written in heaven. After all, they won't be doing no miracles up in heaven!

What I care about is to have God's character. I want to be like my Jesus. I want to talk like my Jesus talked, I want to walk like my Jesus walked, and I want to live like my Jesus lived. "He that saith he abideth in him ought himself also so to walk, even as he walked" (1 John 2:6). Not too long ago, I woke up groaning and groaning. I wasn't feeling sick either. I believe that I'm just waiting for my adoption papers to be signed, sealed, and delivered!

> *For as many as are led by the Spirit of God, they are the sons of God. For ye have not received the spirit of bondage again to fear; but ye have received the Spirit of adoption, whereby we cry, Abba, Father. The Spirit itself beareth witness with our*

spirit, that we are the children of God: And if children, then heirs; heirs of God, and joint-heirs with Christ; if so be that we suffer with him, that we may be also glorified together.

For I reckon that the sufferings of this present time are not worthy to be compared with the glory which shall be revealed in us. For the earnest expectation of the creature waiteth for the manifestation of the sons of God. For the creature was made subject to vanity, not willingly, but by reason of him who hath subjected the same in hope, Because the creature itself also shall be delivered from the bondage of corruption into the glorious liberty of the children of God.

For we know that the whole creation groaneth and travaileth in pain together until now. And not only they, but ourselves also, which have the firstfruits of the Spirit, even we ourselves groan within ourselves, waiting for the adoption, to wit, the redemption of our body.

Romans 8:14–23

Behold, what manner of love the Father hath bestowed upon us, that we should be called the sons of God: therefore the world knoweth us not, because it knew him not. Beloved, now are we the sons of God, and it doth not yet appear what we shall be: but we know that, when he shall appear, we shall be like him; for we shall see him as he is. And every man that hath this hope in him purifieth himself, even as he is pure.

1 John 3:1–3

We can see how bad of a shape this world is in. There are so many discouraged and confused people because of what is taking place. We need to allow God to change us so that we can be a light to them and let them know that they can become a son or daughter of the Most High God!

Chapter 7

Nothing Shall Separate Me from the Love of God

> *"And thou shalt love the Lord thy God with all thy heart, and with all thy soul, and with all thy mind, and with all thy strength: this is the first commandment" (Mark 12:30). "And now, Israel, what doth the Lord thy God require of thee, but to fear the Lord thy God, to walk in all his ways, and to love him, and to serve the Lord thy God with all thy heart and with all thy soul"*
>
> Deuteronomy 10:12

Since this commandment is the most important commandment, and since God is love and God's love is pure, I realized that only God can give us the pure, genuine love that we need in order to be able to share His love with others. When I began going through that three-year horrible trial, I got honest with God, and I told Him bluntly that I didn't fear Him!

I told Him that I didn't love Him the way that I should. I also let Him know that I didn't even reverence Him, and I told Him that I didn't even feel Him! I was also tired of quoting the scripture, "Greater is He that is in me than he that is in the world," when the truth was that I couldn't feel a solitary thing!

I just got fed up, and I let God know that I wasn't feeling anything greater on the inside of me. I also let Him know that reading His Word was like me eating stale toast, and I wanted to know why. Because that was the honest truth, and let me tell you, God does respond to truth! And I'm finding out more and more that truth will definitely set one free! I thank God that He answered me!

God really doesn't mind us having fits. Sometimes for us to just sit there and be quiet while we don't feel anything at all will not get us anywhere. It's kind of how so many quiet marriages are today, and that's why many couples feel loveless and numb. I knew that it was definitely time for me to get real with God! I used to have that intimate relationship with God, and I would weep in my prayer time, but sadly, that intimacy with God got lost somewhere, and I was ever determined to be intimate with Him again!

Many parents don't have time to spend time with their children and show them love and affection; instead, they will give them expensive clothes, toys, and electronics and want to call that love. And as they grow older they sit there and wonder why their children aren't around. They wonder why their children don't have time for them and why they have become so distant and cold.

Wives become the maids, and husbands become the ATM machines. People have lost that loving feeling simply because they were not taught to give to each other, and they certainly didn't learn the meaning of sacrifice. Sadly, many people feel that love is just about getting everything that they want or what they think that they want! Well, the same goes with God.

Many people feel that God is a genie in a bottle! We call on God when we need Him and not because we really want Him. "God, just get the job done already, and don't make me wait lest I stop going to church!" But then when something bad happens, we want to cry out, "Why did God allow this to happen to me?"

We have forgotten the meaning of giving. After all, we have a right to be blessed! I want a new home! I want a bigger plane! I want a new wife/husband and new kids too! Bless God! Then when people actually get what they asked for, we often hear them cry out and say, "God, why did you give me this wife/husband/child?" The Bible says that "we love [God] because He first loved us" (1 John 4:19).

We simply cannot love the way God loves unless we truly understand God's love, and until we truly love God, we cannot love others with the love of God. In order for us to walk in the love of God, we must first seek how to love Him as He commands us to, which is with all our heart, mind, soul, and strength. The Bible says nothing can separate us from the love of God, and that means that we are so in love with God that we cannot be separated from loving Him no matter what tragedy may come our way.

> *Who shall separate us from the love of Christ? shall tribulation, or distress, or persecution, or famine, or nakedness, or peril, or sword? For I am persuaded, that neither death, nor life, nor angels, nor principalities, nor powers, nor things present, nor things to come, Nor height, nor depth, nor any other creature, shall be able to separate us from the love of God, which is in Christ Jesus our Lord.*
>
> Romans 8:35–39

Some people want to interpret that verse as saying that nothing shall separate God from loving us, but when we read the whole scripture, then we must realize that the scripture was talking about us loving God. God already showed us how much He loves us by sending His Son to suffer the beatings as He was mocked and ridiculed and then dying on the cross for us. There is no greater love than that.

It makes me think about the shooting that took place in Columbine High School in Littleton, Colorado, on April 20th, 1999. I heard that the killer had asked the seventeen-year-old girl, Cassie Bernall, if she believed in God, and she, fully knowing that the end result could be death, didn't hesitate to answer him with a resounding yes. The killer shot her and killed her because of it.

Years later after the shooting, I was sitting in church, and I heard someone on the pulpit talking about that incident. This person was saying that anything was possible and that something like that could happen in the church that I had been attending. When she spoke those words, I really had to think about what I would do if I was faced with that situation.

Would I deny God? Or would I boldly and fearlessly do what that young girl did? I really didn't know what I would do, and that right there scared me in a bad way! I knew that for me to feel that way was not good, and I wanted to know why I was feeling that way and why I was so unassured of what I would do. I stated earlier that I realized that I didn't love God like I should.

I remember the time that I first gave my life to God. I used to be so in love with Him. I would always talk with Him, and I remember how I started reading the Bible, and it was so refreshing! I used to fall asleep with my tape recorder playing a tape of the Bible in my ear. We had a wonderful relationship! I did not go to church at that time; it was just Him and me!

But then I started going to a church, and I loved it! It was a megachurch. I would get so blessed at this church because the anointing was so strong. There were times that the anointing was so strong that when people would run to the front, they would literally fall out in the Spirit before they even got to the front! I felt that I was in the right place because I loved being in the awesome presence of God!

But then I got so involved in the church that I forgot about God, and our relationship began to diminish. I believe that I fell more in love with the church that I had been attending and less in love with God. I was in love with all the activities that they had at the church, and I fell in love with my title! I had lost my first love.

I used to put my trust in anyone who was anointed, and I was in love with listening to preachers with a big name! Later, I realized that just because someone is anointed does not mean that they don't have their faults. Christians will tell other Christians that they love them, but do their actions follow? Do their actions speak louder than their words?

I have been reading the book of Songs of Solomon, and it describes the love that the Shulamite woman had for the king. It also describes the love that the king had for the Shulamite woman. God is comparing this to the love that He has for us. I didn't understand what it was to love someone with that kind of love.

I know that God's love is great, and I wanted to love God that great, but I couldn't even fathom someone having that kind of love for anyone else. That love is quite deep. We say that we love people, our children, our wives, our husbands, and our mothers, yet when they hurt us, suddenly we find that our love for them diminishes.

We say we love God, and we really want to, but I just knew there was something keeping me from loving Him like I really should, and that was because I didn't really know God. I was weeping today because I know that there are so many people who don't have that kind of love for one another, and many of them are churchgoers. The sad part is that they don't realize it.

People who visit church may see happy people praising God, dancing, and rejoicing, and they want to be a part of that because it looks wonderful! But when they decide to join the church, they find out that it's not all that they thought it was cut out to be. They just jumped into this thing called church and did what I did. "We are happy people; yes, we are!" But the fact is that nobody wants to talk to nobody!

I remember one time when the church that I was attending was having a small carnival outside. I thought that it was going to be fun, but when I showed up, I tried talking to some people, but nobody really cared to talk to me. I'm a leader, and I thought I had friends! Hello? So I left; I figured what was the point of standing there alone! It was such a weird feeling to see Christian people like that. There was no fellowship, there was no fruit-bearing, and there was no love whatsoever!

People who come to visit a church are looking for something different than what they experience in the world. They want to feel like they are a part of something. They want to feel accepted and loved. Many times, people who come to church to receive healing may hear the preacher say, "You must forgive and get over it!" They really don't need someone screaming in their ears; instead, they need to hear that God heals the brokenhearted.

When a person tries to forgive someone would be the same as a person who tries to love someone that they don't have feelings for. To forgive someone who has hurt you so badly is not something that a person can do on their own. I know that the Bible says that we must forgive others, or God won't forgive us. But just because the Bible says it doesn't make it easy for us to do. Even though it is scriptural, preachers need to understand that people have a grudge for a reason.

There are many reasons that people get hurt. They may have been hurt by someone's actions; they may have been raped, or maybe their loved one died or was murdered. They may have been badly beaten by someone or mentally beaten. The Bible says, "The love of God is shed abroad our Hearts by the Holy Ghost" (Romans 5:5).

Not only will it take God's Holy Spirit to bring complete healing to a person's broken heart, but the Holy Spirit can also instill God's genuine love in us for us to love God and others. God's Word is Spirit and life, and if we want to receive complete healing, we must be in His Word.

God's Spirit will help us to forgive, and He will also help us to love those who hurt us, that is, if we truly want Him to. That does not mean that we need to spend time with a person who wants to hurt us, but we will be able to release that person over to God and pray for them. When I used to hold grudges for certain people, I felt miserable!

Having unforgiveness is like being in a very dark place. It felt like I was being tied down with heavy chains, but when I decided to let go of my hatred and believe God for my healing, even as painful as it was for me to do, then God started the healing process in my life, and I was able to forgive others, and those chains were broken off of me! Thank You, Jesus!

When I began seeking God, then I found myself falling in love with Him. I realized that you really can't love someone whom you really don't know. So many marriages break up because they really didn't take the time that they needed for them to really get to know each other. They may have felt that loving feeling in the beginning as I did with God, but then they began to slowly drift apart. I felt the presence of God many times than I can number and even fell out in the Spirit, and yet I didn't know Him.

I knew what He felt like, but I didn't really know who He was until I began reading about Him in the Bible. And when I started doing that, then I found out who God really is. I also found out what God could do. I also found out how to please Him. When someone that you don't know makes a promise to you, it's hard to believe them. But as I got to know God and even read about what He has done, then my faith in Him began to grow, and my love for Him continues to grow because of it.

I can now say that I would gladly die for my Jesus, and I can confidently say that nothing shall separate me from the love of God. He truly is my all and all! And now I know that if I was ever faced with a situation of death and some crazy maniac asked me the question, "Do you love God?" I can say without hesitations that I know that I would respond, "*Yes*!"

We need to realize that these most certainly are the last days that we live in, and there will be many tests and trials. We can certainly see how the economy is doing! The death tolls are rising daily, and persecution of the church is already happening. This is all Bible prophecy, and the Anti-Christ is getting ready to show up. That great getting up day is coming...fare thee well!

So we must ask ourselves if we are going to continue to love God through all of this. This should not leave you with a question mark in your head as it did mine. Don't wait till it happens to you, but make sure that you know that you know that you know the answer is *yes*! Can you say that you honestly love the Lord with all your heart, soul, and all your might? Be very sure...

Chapter 8

The Fear of the Lord Is Only the Beginning

When I started reading the Bible through, then I began to see myself. I could not believe how much of a complainer I was, and not only that, but I was able to see how unthankful I was! I began to see so many things that I was doing that were unpleasing to God. That's because I was living after the flesh.

So I went to God and asked Him why I was so unhappy and why I didn't have any peace when that was what the Bible promised me. I asked God what I was doing wrong, and I got answers. That was when I found out that the answers were all in the Bible! I must say that I didn't like the answers that I got either! That's because when I got the answers, then I came to find out how unpleasing to God that I really was.

I found out that even little things like me complaining were quite annoying and offensive to God. I read how God destroyed many people who complained. "And when the people complained, it displeased the Lord: and the Lord heard it; and his anger was kindled; and the fire of the Lord burnt among them, and consumed them that were in the uttermost parts of the camp" (Numbers 11:1).

I must say that scripture was quite a wake-up call for me! Once again people are really destroyed for the lack of knowledge, and I know that I was being destroyed for that very reason! We know that God loves us so much and that He's really not into killing us; however, the Bible says that God has killed many people because they disobeyed Him and because they were unthankful.

This may come as quite a shock for those who don't read the Bible, but if they would read the Bible through, then they would know. There are so many people who just want to read the good part of the Bible, and I admit that I used to do the same. I just wanted to know about my promises! But when I began to read the Bible through was when I found out that there really is more to God than I hear preached from the pulpit.

In order for us to receive God's promise, we need to know who God is. We also need to know what pleases Him, and we certainly need to know what does not please Him. We also need to know what God is capable of doing to those who He is not pleased with. Some of you may think that God's wrath was just for the Old Testament, but if you read, you will find out that is not the case at all.

The fear of the *Lord* really is just the beginning of wisdom. We want to believe that God is someone who loves us so much that He will never bring harm to us because we are Christians, but when I read the book of Job, I see that that is not altogether true. It was God who allowed Satan to attack Job.

God removed His hedge from Job so that Satan was able to freely get into Job's life and make his life a living nightmare. Why? Well, I'm learning that God does test us. I don't believe that anyone likes tests! If we never get tested, then how will we know where we truly stand? God also commanded Abraham to kill his beloved child—another test! God was going to kill Moses for not circumcising his sons! (Exodus 4:24–26).

We can also read in the New Testament how God also killed a couple of people because they lied to the Holy Spirit (Acts 5:1–10). The Bible says, "For the wrath of God is revealed from heaven against all ungodliness and unrighteousness of men, who hold the truth in unrighteousness" (Romans 1:18). We also know that there will be a judgment day, and we all will be judged by God.

> *When the Son of man shall come in his glory, and all the holy angels with him, then shall he sit upon the throne of his glory: And before him shall be gathered all nations: and he shall separate them one from another, as a shepherd divideth his sheep from the goats: And he shall set the sheep on his right hand, but the goats on the left.*

> *Then shall the King say unto them on his right hand, Come, ye blessed of my Father, inherit the kingdom prepared for you from the foundation of the world: Then shall he say also unto them on the left hand, Depart from me, ye cursed, into everlasting fire, prepared for the devil and his angels.*
>
> Matthew 25:31–34, 41

Though the main gospel is not for God to kill anyone, just like pit bulls have it in them to kill, I am finding out shockingly that God also has it in Him to kill. "See now that I, even I, am he, and there is no god with me: I kill, and I make alive; I wound, and I heal: neither is there any that can deliver out of my hand" (Deuteronomy 32:39).

So at any rate, I read about what God doesn't like, and I also read how God blesses those who do what He does like. God even gives us plenty of warnings in the Bible of what He will do if we disobey Him. You can read some of it in the book of Deuteronomy 28. He tells us the blessings that He will give to those who obey Him, and then He tells us the cursings that He will bring upon those who disobey Him.

Then He plainly tells us to choose life because His desire is for us to choose life and not death. When we choose life, the Bible tells us that He will give us life more abundantly. God wants to give us so much more than we can even ask, think, or even comprehend, and yet we can see so many Christian people who are not receiving their blessings.

There are many Christians who lack peace and have no joy whatsoever. We can see how so many families need restoration in their relationships. God wants us to be complete in Him, and He doesn't want us to be lacking in any area of our lives. Sadly, so many people are serving the wrong god because they simply don't know anything about the One True God. Some people only know what they hear preachers say about God.

When we are sick, we go to the doctors, and we pay them money to make us better. We may not even know anything about the doctor but when they prescribe us something, we gladly take what they prescribe. We don't ask questions, but we simply believe the medicine will work for us because the doctor said it would.

We trust the doctor to do the right thing, and yet when it comes to God, we are always hesitant to do what His Word tells us to do in order for us to get better. Why is it so hard for us to trust Him for everything that we need? Why do we trust in a doctor who we don't even know more than we trust God, the One who created us?

I wanted answers, and as I continue to seek His Word, I can honestly say that I am getting them! The Bible tells us to "draw nigh to God and He will draw nigh to [us]" (James 4:8); another verse says, "Call unto me [God] and I will answer thee" (Jeremiah 33:3). Another verse tells us, "Ye have not, because ye ask not" (James 4:2). Some people quote those scriptures so much, and yet they don't seem to hear or see anything from God.

I don't take God's Word lightly. And because I continue to read the Bible every day, I can honestly say that when God speaks to me, there is no confusion whatsoever. I'm falling so head over heels in love with my Jesus! When you love someone so much, then you start feeling what they are feeling, and when they hurt, then you hurt. That's how I'm feeling about God.

I even find myself getting upset when He gets upset. Sometimes when He's upset, I try to calm Him down. Like when it rains and the winds start blowing really, really hard, I will try to calm Him down, but I must admit, I do love hearing Him roar and thunder! It just shows me how strong He is when He roars and speaks in His thunderous voice! What a rush! I know that some people want to blame bad weather on Mother Nature. That's because they don't realize that it's really in Papa's nature to do those things! Get it right!

> *At this also my heart trembleth, and is moved out of his place. Hear attentively the noise of his voice, and the sound that goeth out of his mouth. He directeth it under the whole heaven, and his lightning unto the ends of the earth. After it a voice roareth: he thundereth with the voice of his excellency; and he will not stay them when his voice is heard.*
>
> *God thundereth marvellously with his voice; great things doeth he, which we cannot comprehend. For he saith to the snow, Be*

thou on the earth; likewise to the small rain, and to the great rain of his strength.

Job 37:1–6

Out of the south cometh the whirlwind: and cold out of the north. By the breath of God frost is given: and the breadth of the waters is straitened.

Also by watering he wearieth the thick cloud: he scattereth his bright cloud: And it is turned round about by his counsels: that they may do whatsoever he commandeth them upon the face of the world in the earth. He causeth it to come, whether for correction, or for his land, or for mercy.

Job 37:9–13

You can only appreciate these scriptures when you know God as your Daddy! Keep in mind that just as any father would have their child obey them, we must also obey God lest we feel His wrath! And let me tell you from experience, that is no fun at all! God does chastise those whom He loves (Hebrews 12:6). You will learn who God really is as you read the Bible through, and you will learn what His attributes are.

Some people want to think that God is this furry creature who cuddles with us and loves us no matter what we do or how we may act, but the Bible explains things about God quite differently. The Bible says, "The fear of the Lord is the beginning of wisdom: and the knowledge of the holy is understanding" (Proverbs 9:10). We will know and understand God when we begin fear Him.

The Bible tells us to fear God for a reason, and there are so many scriptures that speak of the many benefits that we will have when we do. Yet today, the fear of the Lord seems to be obsolete! Fearing God is kind of like when we fear policemen or a judge who will bring forth judgment. We certainly don't want to do or say anything that would get either one of them mad at us.

If we didn't have a court system that punished us for our actions, then we really wouldn't care if we passed a red light, or if we went over the speed limit, or even if we shot somebody who cut us off on the road. Today, we can see that most people don't fear even that; instead, they have a "catch me if you can" attitude! Sadly, we can see that there are a lot of people who have that same attitude with God, and then they wonder why they suffer the way they do.

Some people don't believe in God's wrath, but we can see all the things that are happening now are what God said in His Word that He would do to those who reject Him or His Word. Not too many preachers want to preach that truth, but only the truth will make people free. God brought harm to those who opposed His people, Israel! When we look at what God did to Pharaoh of Egypt, I must say that God's payback was no treat for the Egyptians!

How long, ye simple ones, will ye love simplicity? and the scorners delight in their scorning, and fools hate knowledge? Turn you at my reproof: behold, I will pour out my spirit unto you, I will make known my words unto you. Because I have called, and ye refused; I have stretched out my hand, and no man regarded;

But ye have set at nought all my counsel, and would none of my reproof: I also will laugh at your calamity; I will mock when your fear cometh; When your fear cometh as desolation, and your destruction cometh as a whirlwind; when distress and anguish cometh upon you. Then shall they call upon me, but I will not answer; they shall seek me early, but they shall not find me:

For that they hated knowledge and did not choose the fear of the Lord: They would none of my counsel: they despised all my reproof. Therefore shall they eat of the fruit of their own way, and be filled with their own devices. For the turning away of the simple shall slay them, and the prosperity of fools shall destroy them. But whoso hearkeneth unto me shall dwell safely, and shall be quiet from fear of evil.

Proverbs 1:22–32

When we reject the Word of God, then we are rejecting God, and if we don't have to fear God, then why should we even bother being good? Let me just go hit the next nightclub, get drunk, and party hard because God doesn't care, and He will bless me in any way that I act!

I remember when I had a *"God-fearing"* experience. Whew! I can say that it was a very horrifying one! One time when I was praying, I was asking God to give me "the fear of the Lord" only because I knew that I didn't have it. A few days later, I needed to go to the bank, which was a few minutes away from my house.

It looked like a beautiful day out, sunshine and all. It certainly did not look like it was going to storm. But then when I was driving home from the bank, all of a sudden, it started getting very dark out. It was around 3 p.m., and suddenly, and out of nowhere, the winds started to blow very hard! Then I saw big branches and big objects that came out of nowhere, flying right in front of my windshield!

After that, I saw huge lightning strikes on the left side of me and on the right side! Then on the left side of me, I saw another lightning strike an apartment sign, and the sign started on fire! Boy, was I ever frightened! Then I remembered that I had asked God to give me His fear, and I knew that He was answering my prayer!

We really must be careful of what we pray for! So, then I was praying for God to help me make it home, and thankfully He answered that prayer! We must understand that to fear God is an advantage for us. If you search the Bible, then you will know why. When bad things happen, we often want to start blaming the devil, but as I have been reading the Bible, I realize that the devil can do things to us only when God gives him the permission to.

We can give the devil permission ourselves by rejecting or disobeying God. The bottom line is when we are not serving God, then we are serving the devil. "Know ye not, that to whom ye yield yourselves servants to obey, his servants ye are to whom ye obey; whether of sin unto death, or of obedience unto righteousness?" (Romans 6:16).

There have been many times that I had to repent to God for giving the devil too much credit. God is the One who created this earth, and it all belongs to God, not the devil. When we are serving God, He is in control of everything that goes on in our lives. You will only understand God's nature when you begin seeking Him.

So many times in the Bible, I read about the fear of the Lord and how God wants us to fear Him, and yet, sadly, I hear so many preachers who are not preaching that. Instead, they say that for us to fear God is like a papa fear, or like one would fear their father, but as I read the Bible, I can see that is not the truth. A Father wouldn't kill his son for disobeying Him, and God has killed many people for disobeying Him.

We can start from the flood, where He destroyed the whole world except a very few. The Bible says that God will be a father to those who fear Him (Psalm 103:13). I love this chapter! Since Jesus is the Word manifested and the Word is God, then when we leave out some of the Word and think that Jesus is separate from His Word, then we are leaving out a part of God.

Sadly, so many preachers may want to say good things for everybody to hear that will make them feel happy, but when they do that, they are leaving out the key to being happy, joyful, fruit-bearing, loving, and true Christians. Just like a father and mother would want to see their children happy and they want to say everything that will make their children happy, but even fathers and mothers must correct their children and train them to go the right way lest...their children don't.

Unfortunately, so many parents feel that their child is happy by doing whatever they want to do and by them having whatever they want, and they seem to be okay with that. Some parents feel that correcting their child is a bad thing because they feel that they are hurting them. That's why many children grow up thinking that is what life is about and they feel that they can have anything they want and they never have to do anything to get it.

Just look all around. Many businesses can't seem to find workers to hire because there are few people who want to work! We can also look at all the crimes that are taking place among kids! Very, very sad indeed! But once again the Bible tells us differently. It says, "He that spareth his rod hateth his son, and he that loveth him chastised him betimes" (Proverbs 13:24). "Chasten thy son while there is hope, and let not thy soul spare for his crying" (Proverbs 19:18). God is a God of correction.

"But if ye be without chastisement, whereof all are partakers, then are ye bastards, and not sons" (Hebrews 12:8). "In this the children of God are manifest, and the children of the devil: whosoever doeth not righteousness is not of God, neither he that loveth not his brother" (1 John 3:10). These are scriptures that probably many Christians don't know are in the Bible, and they wonder why they suffer.

It's really not hard to see who is walking and talking like the devil and those who aren't, and we should pray for those people who aren't. The Bible also tells us that we must also turn away from them as well. That may be a little shocking for you to hear!

> *This know also, that in the last days perilous times shall come. For men shall be lovers of their own selves, covetous, boasters, proud, blasphemers, disobedient to parents, unthankful, unholy, Without natural affection, trucebreakers, false accusers, incontinent, fierce, despisers of those that are good, Traitors, heady, highminded, lovers of pleasures more than lovers of God;*
>
> *Having a form of godliness, but denying the power thereof: from such turn away. For of this sort are they which creep into houses, and lead captive silly women laden with sins, led away with divers lusts, Ever learning, and never able to come to the knowledge of the truth.*
>
> 2 Timothy 3:1–7

These are the last days, and people need to be prepared and put on their armor!

We can read that there is so much more to fearing God. The book of Proverbs talks a lot about fearing God. Proverbs is a book of wisdom. It was written by the wisest man on the planet, next to Jesus. If anyone is praying for wisdom, I suggest that they read a chapter a day from the book of Proverbs since there are only thirty-one chapters. I sure wish there were more!

When a person fears someone, they don't want to upset them lest they end up getting messed up by them! Just think about being at work; when the boss walks in, you will see everyone in the room get quiet and start working. You definitely wouldn't want your boss to see you playing around less!

To fear God is to understand that there are consequences to our actions as with fearing your boss, the policeman, or the judge. Though God is merciful and full of compassion, the Bible says that He is merciful to them who fear Him (Psalm 103:17). Many churches got it all wrong by thinking that it's okay for people to do what they want even if it hurts God's feelings.

And many leaders will tell people who sin that they don't have to worry about anything. I have to say that I have learned differently, not only from reading the Bible but also from my experiences. We can read the Bible and see how many people got killed from hurting God's feelings because they worshipped other gods and did wickedly.

I thank God for the Bible and His Holy Spirit, who not only teaches us how to live good but also gives us His grace and His power to help us do good while we are living on this planet. After King Solomon built the house of the Lord and brought the ark of the covenant to the house, then he prayed to God.

If you read 2 Chronicles chapter 6, you will see how he was saying that after God punishes them for their sin and God afflicts them by shutting up the heaven with no rain or with locust or mildew or sickness, then if the people repent and return to Him with all their heart and with all their soul, he asked God to please hear from heaven their prayer and forgive them.

"That they may fear thee, to walk in thy ways, so long as they live in the land which thou gavest unto our fathers" (2 Chronicles 6:31). Then God answered:

> *If I shut up heaven and there be no rain, or if I command the locust to devour the land, or if I send pestilence among my people: if my people which are called by my name shall humble*

themselves, and pray and seek my face, and turn from their wicked ways, then I will hear from heaven, and will forgive their sins, and will heal their land.

2 Chronicles 7:13–14

This is God talking! People don't believe that God does this kind of stuff! People really need to wake up and get to know this God who they say they serve. They need to know that God is not a cuddly teddy bear and realize that He is a God! "And unto man he said, Behold, the fear of the Lord, that is wisdom; and to depart from evil is understanding" (Job 28:28). "The secret of the Lord is with them that fear him; and he will shew them his covenant" (Psalm 25:14).

"The angel of the Lord encampeth round about them that fear him, and delivereth them" Psalm 34:7). "The fear of the Lord is to hate evil: pride, and arrogancy, and the evil way, and the froward mouth, do I hate" (Proverbs 8:13). "The fear of the Lord prolongeth days: but the years of the wicked shall be shortened" (Proverbs 10:27). "By humility and the fear of the Lord are riches, and honour, and life" (Proverbs 22:4).

There are so many more verses pertaining to fearing God in the Bible, and we can see the good that comes from fearing Him. To fear God is the key to a successful life, and the great thing is that when we truly fear God, then we don't have to fear anyone or anything else! "O that there were such an heart in them, that they would fear me, and keep all my commandments always, that it might be well with them, and with their children for ever!" (Deuteronomy 5:29).

We should realize that we don't know everything, and there will always be somebody who knows more than we do. There is only one person who knows everything, and that's the One who created us, this world, and the universe. God created it perfectly because He is perfect, and when we choose to serve Him, then we need God's instructions in order for us to live a prosperous, successful, peaceful, and joyful life.

God's will above everything is for us to be prosperous and in good health, and whatever He tells us or commands us to do will only lead us there. After all, who doesn't want that? When you get a job, you have rules to go by. Your boss doesn't give you rules to make you a slave per se, but instead, they give you rules so the company can be successful and so that you can earn money to survive.

Today there are many preachers who say that you don't have to obey God's commandments because they want to excuse the actions of the people in order to please the people. So they will tell everyone that they just need to confess Jesus as their Lord and they don't have to do anything else. They don't mention anything about making God the *Lord* of their life.

That's why we see many Christian people who are sick and many who continue to struggle; they never seem to get ahead no matter what they do. We can see how so many people are losing their families and their homes; it's just because they don't know better. In other words, they don't have a boss to direct them on what to do. They don't read their Bible simply because they weren't told that they needed to.

A good leader leads us into good things, and God is a great leader who wants to lead us into great things, but if we don't listen, then we really shouldn't expect too much. When we really know God, then we will truly fear Him, and that's when we can expect blessings. And when we fear God, we won't be quick to do wrong, just as we wouldn't be quick to do wrong at our job unless we don't have one!

Before I read the Bible through, I never really knew that it talked about fearing God, simply because I didn't know God...period! I encourage you to read these chapters: Job 38; Psalm 18:11–15, 148; Isaiah 30. These chapters are describing God's greatness. It's so silly for a person to think that we don't need to fear the One who can stop us from breathing or stop our heart from beating at any given moment! God is to be feared and reverenced simply because He is *God Almighty*! "And fear not them which kill the body, but are not able to kill the soul: but rather fear him which is able to destroy both soul and body in hell" (Matthew 10:28).

Chapter 9

Put Not Your Trust in Man

One time, when I was watching TV, I saw Michael Jackson in an interview with someone. This person was asking Michael something like, "Who do you trust with your money?" and the answer that Michael gave was quite a sad one. He said something like, "There are those who steal a lot from me, and then there are those who don't steal quite as much from me, and the ones that steal less are the ones that I put in charge of my money."

What a sad statement indeed! Too many people are looking for someone to place their trust in, and sadly they end up getting great disappointments. Been there, done that! As I have been reading the Bible, the light of God shines ever so brightly, and many times, I can see right through people. It's kind of like I have a special lightbulb on me. I must say that it's not always a good feeling when I see stuff, but on the other hand, the more stuff that I see, the more I learn not to put my trust in a man or woman for that matter.

Anyone who lives in a fleshly body can get in the flesh at any given moment; just watch them at a ball game! I once heard a well-known preacher say that when they wake up, they get into prayer and they have the most wonderful time with God, but once they get out of their prayer closet, there's a battle waiting ahead of them.

"Who ate my slice of sweet potato pie?" "Where in the world did this bill come from?" "Why in the world is the kitchen a mess when I just cleaned it?" We want to believe that stuff doesn't happen to the spiritual elite. I don't really know if a person really gets to a point where they can just be calm about everything. I sure wish I could!

Remember that the apostle Paul said that he had to die every single day. There's a reason that he said that. If you know someone who wakes up all smiley face and never gets upset at anything, then I suggest that you cling on to the person and find their secret! I also believe that there are those who have the fruit of the spirit who actually live the fruitful life, but I don't know too many of them.

I also know people who are like that, who get tired and worn out from doing so much for others because they don't know how to say no to anyone... people really need to know how to say "no!" God doesn't want us to put our trust in anyone but Him. He never gets tired or worn out from doing things for us, and you can be sure that He will never get tired of hearing from us.

When someone came and told Moses that other people were prophesying and they told Moses to stop them, then Moses said that He wished that all the Lord's people were prophets and wished that God would put His Spirit on everyone. "Now the man Moses was very meek, above all the men which were upon the face of the earth" (Numbers 12:3). Moses had a lot of love for the people. He was one of a kind!

"And there arose not a prophet since in Israel like unto Moses, whom the Lord knew face to face" (Deuteronomy 34:10). God wanted to destroy the people of Israel and start over with Moses, but Moses had so much love that he wouldn't have it.

> *And the Lord said unto Moses, I have seen this people, and, behold, it is a stiffnecked people:*
>
> *Now therefore let me alone, that my wrath may wax hot against them, and that I may consume them: and I will make of thee a great nation. Yet now, if thou wilt forgive their sin—; and if not, blot me, I pray thee, out of thy book which thou hast written.*
>
> Exodus 32:9–10, 32

We can see why God chose him to lead the people out of Egypt.

There is a reason that the Bible tells us not to put our trust in man. "It is better to trust in the Lord than to put confidence in man. Put not your trust in princes, nor in the son of man, in whom there is no help" (Psalm 118:8, 146:3). So many people get hurt and are wounded because of a person that they put their trust in and were let down.

Now I know without a shadow of a doubt that no man is perfect, nor can they do everything perfectly, and that's the way that I look at every single person that I meet, whether they have accomplished great things or not. However, I don't want you to mix up imperfection with sin. When I say there is no perfect person, I'm talking about people who make mistakes.

I don't want you to think that I am talking about people sinning when I talk about people not being perfect. You may not believe this, but there are people who don't have to sin every day! Just about every day, I am faced with things that I need to make decisions about, and I have no clue what to do. And there are people who may have to deal with their family members and may make the wrong choices because they just don't know what to do.

Husbands make mistakes with their wives and vice versa. "Why in the world would you give me a vacuum cleaner for my anniversary!" That kind of stuff. I've learned to accept everyone for who they are because I realize that I am just as imperfect as everyone else. I still make plenty of mistakes because I don't know everything.

There are many times that I am asking myself, *Why did I do that?* Or, *Why didn't I do that?* Or I may get upset and say things that I should have never said. Sometimes I buy something that I should have never bought. People forget to check the oil in their car. People may marry the wrong person.

The list can go on and on. We all make mistakes simply because we don't know everything. I can say one big mistake that I see many people make, and that is leaving their vehicles unlocked! I'm sure we have all heard many stories about that. Just go on the Nextdoor app. It's really getting bad, y'all!

I surely don't put my trust in me, and I wouldn't want anyone else to put their trust in me either—trust me! I need to kill my flesh every single day! When we yield over to our flesh, it will never stop talking, and no matter who you are, if you are wearing a body suit of flesh, it will always be screaming out, "I want more!" This thing is never ever ever ever satisfied!

The Bible tells us that there is a war going on in us. "For we wrestle not against flesh and blood, but against principalities, against powers, against the rulers of the darkness of this world, against spiritual wickedness in high places" (Ephesians 6:12). That means we are always fighting! We need to continually fight the good fight of faith (1 Timothy 6:2). A fight is a fight!

I've learned that people who have set their mind on something, no matter what you or anybody else says, you will not be able to change their mind. So many people that I know do crazy things and will continue to do crazy things. I have tried to change the way that some people think.

I tried to stop some people from doing crazy things, but I had to learn the hard way, and I realized that nothing I did or said worked! "He loves me!" "Then why does he beat you?" "Why doesn't he get a job?" "Why does he talk to you like that?" "I can't pay my rent!" "Then why did you just buy all those clothes that you don't need?"

Then I realized that no one could change my thoughts no matter what they said or did! I'm the only one who can change my way of thinking. We may feel like we know someone who we can really confide in, but I realized that half the time people aren't really listening to us anyway; a lot of the times, it is because their mind is always going!

Now that I'm getting closer to God, sometimes I can see what other people are thinking, and I'm blown away! But then, when I look at my own mind and see how messed up it is, I can understand why other people's minds are just as messed up! There have been times when a person is talking to me, and I will admit that sometimes I'm not listening to them.

There were times that I was staring at their makeup or looking at what they were wearing. There were times that I was thinking about what I was going to cook for dinner. There have been times when I was looking at someone else and I was not even paying attention to the person who was talking to me. But when people do that to me, I think that is so rude, and now I am able to relate with their rudeness!

I'm not saying that it's right to do that, but now that I am aware of it, I am definitely working on that! When your brain talks, sometimes you can't help but listen to it...especially because it talks so loud! It's kind of scary knowing that people's minds travel a hundred miles an hour just thinking so much. I don't like it, and I'm determined to be free from these thoughts, and sometimes they really wear me out!

We try so hard to figure things out, and we end up more stressed out and full of worries, but Jesus is saying, "Just give it to me and relax!" The Bible says, "Come unto me, all ye that labour and are heavy laden, and I will give you rest. Take my yoke upon you, and learn of me; for I am meek and lowly in heart: and ye shall find rest unto your souls. For my yoke is easy, and my burden is light" (Matthew 11:28–30).

We can see how many great anointed preachers have fallen because they listened to other people. Nobody can say that they are untouchable. If a person is living, breathing, walking, or talking, then they can be deceived. The Bible says, "Except the Lord shortened the days that no flesh shall be saved, but for the elect's sakes those days shall be shortened" (Mark 13:20). Now that is a scary thought!

A person who thinks that they know everything is a dangerous person. We can clearly see the way things are going and how so many people are losing their minds, from the people in the White House to the elite and educated people, and we certainly can't leave out people in the churches! And because of that, people just don't know what or who to believe anymore! That's why I choose to only believe in the One who knows everything!

Jesus is all I need, want, and desire! God has proven time and time again that His ways are perfect, and He surely knows how to direct my steps! I do love Him so very much! After reading the Bible through year after year, it made me realize how much my thoughts stink, and I realize that I really don't know anything! If I'm in a classroom and I have a question, I don't want to ask another student for the answer, but instead, I want to go directly to the teacher.

It doesn't matter to me how anointed someone may be or even how smart they are; I'd way much rather go to my Jesus for the answers! He is my teacher, and He always has all the right answers! I'm not saying that I can't learn from anyone else by any means because I am always learning from people, and I encourage people to learn from others and get educated, but when it comes to asking about what I should do or about my problems, then I go to God!

Famous people can look around and see the crowds of people who are gathering around to see them when they are successful and are doing well, and then they can see who the crowds really are if they should fail miserably. The crowds loved them at first because they felt like anyone who was famous was perfect or great.

Many people today measure their success by the crowds who are following them, and yet Jesus only had twelve disciples. Sadly, out of the twelve, one of them was a traitor who failed Him miserably! The other eleven scattered when things got rough for Jesus. And even though His disciples walked with Jesus for three years, they still had their faults.

Why do I love Jesus so much? Because He first loved me. I know that He will never leave me either. And as I continue to give Him my life and my time, I know that He will always be there for me. He will never have an excuse as to why He doesn't have time for me, but instead He gets thrilled just to hear my voice, and might I add that He is such a good listener! God will always come first in my life because He's the One that leads me, and He helps me to live out this thing called life!

Chapter 10

Freedom from People's Opinions

I remember another time when I was watching TV, and as I was scrolling through the channels, I saw Whitney Houston talking on a talk show. She was in an interview with someone, and she was saying how she was determined to make her marriage work no matter what. She said that she really wanted to prove to the people that her marriage would work, and that was why she stayed with her husband.

Not too long after that, I heard her talking on several other talk shows about what a nightmare her marriage was. She was also talking about how she wanted to live a normal life; she was saying that she wanted to dress down and wear blue jeans. I guess there are people who tell famous people how to live, dress, and act. Basically, she was pressured into living a lie. Peer pressure can do that, ya know!

There are many people who live by the opinions of the crowds, elite, or whatever, and yet we hear how so many of the elite and famous people's lives are one big mess! Too often people try to live how they see other people live, and they try to do what other people do because they believe that will bring them happiness. They believe that the people who they try to imitate are happy. I remember those days all right!

When I was younger, I was very beautiful. I'm not trying to brag about myself, and I know that the genes in no doubt came from my dad and mom, but I believe that beautiful-looking people have it hard because they feel like they have to look perfect at all times. That's how I felt. Even though I was beautiful on the outside, I will admit that I was not beautiful on the inside!

Sometimes when I see people who are beautiful, I can sense them feeling that way. They're always checking their hair or looking in their small mirror just to make sure that they look just right. If I looked in the mirror and I saw one hair out of place, then I couldn't even think straight because I would be wondering how I was going to fix my hair perfectly! Vanity…vanity, that's all it is!

The reason that I wanted to always look my best was that I always cared about what other people thought about me, or you could say it was because of what I felt like other people thought about me. I used to be so conscious of what everybody else thought. I would feel bad if I just had one little wrinkle spot on my skirt or if I wore shoes that maybe didn't go perfectly with my outfit.

It was so bad that I would even wonder when I sat down if I sat down the right way. I was always wondering what other people were thinking about me! I wanted to fit in so badly and just be like what I thought was perfect. I now realize that people really could care less about how I looked!

I used to watch people in movies, and I would watch how people acted. I would try to act like them because I thought they were so perfect. But as time went on, I realized that all people are just normal people, yes, even the ones on TV! I remember how I used to watch how people acted with other people, and I would always try to imitate them.

I would sit there and totally admire someone who looked like they had it all together until I heard just how miserable they really were. Looks really can be deceiving! People would think that my dogs were adorable because they were little and ever so cute, and they looked so sweet. I would tell them that they were quite deceived by thinking that!

Though my dogs looked sweet and innocent from afar, if you got close to them, you would see their true colors! One time I went to the church to pick something up, and I brought my dog with me. When I got there, one of the leaders saw him, and she started telling me how cute he was until he started growling at her! I told her that my dogs needed to go to a deliverance service!

People tend to think that people with money are happy and because they can buy whatever they want, they really got it all together. I remember one time when I was on a beautiful cruise ship, and I remember how I felt like my legs were getting cellulite. My legs didn't have one ounce of cellulite, but for some strange reason, I believed they did.

I was in my early twenties, and I have to say that my legs were perfect at that time…notice I said "were!" But at that time, my mind was so tormented by thinking that I had cellulite. I felt so bad to the point that when I wore my swimming suit, I would wear a long scarf to cover my legs because I felt that someone would notice something that wasn't even there!

It was so bad to the point that I ordered expensive products for cellulite! I was obsessed! Later in life I realized that the people whom I was concerned with who I thought were looking at my non-cellulite legs were not perfect people either. Some of the people whom I was concerned with seeing me were heavy-set and they had plenty of cellulite.

I realized that those people could care less who saw their belly sticking out of their swimsuit or what people thought of the cellulite on their legs! There were people whom I was worried about seeing my legs who had cracks in their teeth, and they really didn't care what anyone thought! They were just having a sure 'nuff good time on that beautiful ship!

When I realized that I didn't look at them any differently because of their imperfection was when I got set free. People on the cruise ship were having a good time, and yet there I was wallowing in misery because of what I thought other people were thinking about me! How dumb is that? Later on, I wondered why I was so concerned about how I looked to other people.

I thank my God that I'm now free from people's opinions! Now I don't care what people think about me, and I could care less about how I look, for that matter! Sometimes, I will go outside with a wrinkled shirt, mismatched socks, holy shoes, and my hair all sticking up! Sometimes I will even go to the stores that way, and sure enough, nobody says a doggone thing about how I look!

The fact of the matter is that people could really care less about how other people look. And what's funny is now when I go somewhere dressed down, I get more compliments from people than I do when I dress up! People really don't care about how we look unless we are applying for a job or going on a date, and even then, you may be surprised!

People who worry about their looks and spend so much time trying to fix themselves up so perfectly don't realize that they will soon be shriveled up and then one day gone. We are all just a piece of flesh with an expiration date! I remember when I would buy so many clothes for myself! I had so many clothes that I got sick just looking at them in my cluttered closet!

I'm not saying that we should not take care of ourselves, but we don't have to overdo it just to impress others. Our body is the temple of the Holy Spirit, and we should take care of our temple. It's funny how people will act a totally different way when they are around other people to impress them, and they don't even realize it…been there, done that!

When my mom was alive, in her later years, she started losing her hearing, and I had to speak to her in a loud voice, but when I was around other people, I would talk very low to my mother, but when I realized what I was doing, I stopped doing that. I remember when Mom used to love watching this famous gospel singer on TV. She was always smiling, and she looked and talked so very sweetly. As a matter of fact, I thought that she looked like an angel.

My mom would always talk about her to me. I heard that she was going to be at this church close by where I was living at the time, and I decided to go and see her. I bought all her CDs for my mom. But then something happened; while I was in line to buy all her CDs, I saw her acting another way.

She was yelling at her kids really, really loudly, and she was so angry! I wasn't saved at the time, and when I saw that, I was really turned off! I wasn't turned off so much because she was really, really loud with her kids, but I was turned off because she wasn't who my mom and I thought that she was. When I told my mom how she acted, my mom also got turned off, and she stopped listening to her.

People don't realize how it affects others to watch a person act one way when they are in the church performing and then they see a totally different person when they are outside the church. Not only is that a turnoff, but it also gives the church a bad name. I really love watching people who tell on themselves. Now to me, people like that are real!

Most of the time, when people act or put on a show is because they want other people to feel good about them. I'm way over that! I also found out that when I am myself and I tell it like it is, then people are drawn to that. I don't try to hide the way that I am. However, if the way that I act is not lined up with the Word of God, the Holy Spirit will convict me and put me in check! I'm not talking about acting out in the flesh, but I'm talking about being the person that God created us to be.

When we become Christians, we begin going through a growing process. We start out as newborn babies, then toddlers, then teenagers, and so forth. The Bible says, "When I was a child, I spake as a child, I understood as a child, I thought as a child: but when I became a man, I put away childish things" (1 Corinthians 13:11). That's why it's not good for people to take a newborn babe Christian and put them in a high position just because they may be anointed or talented.

We can see that many preachers, singers, and so forth have fallen flat on their faces due to lack of maturity in God; that's simply because they were trying to be or act like somebody that they were not. During our growing process in Christ, we need to be truthful with ourselves and with others. We really don't need to impress anyone.

We must understand that people are people, and there is no difference no matter who they are. We all put our pants on one leg at a time. We don't wake up looking good, but we all need to fix ourselves up every day. Everyone has their problems, and we all have faults! No one is faultless, no matter how spiritual they may be.

We need not to be told how to act like everyone else, whoever everyone else is! Instead, we need to be free from people's opinions and just be ourselves. The job of the pastors and leaders of the church is to teach their congregation how to seek God and teach them how to spend time with God and study His Word.

When people take the time to do that, then God will help them to renew their mind, and He will transform them by His Holy Spirit. The Bible tells us what needs to be changed in us, and as we submit to God, then He will do the rest! He will teach us how to act, walk, talk, live, and everything else on top of that. He will also direct our steps and guide us.

The closer that we get to God, the more He will be able to help us be the person that we were meant to be in Christ Jesus. It really is awesome! Once a person knows God for who He is, they will be more confident, bolder, and wiser, and they will not fear because Christ really is the One who is being formed in us! "My little children, of whom I travail in birth again until Christ be formed in you" (Galatians 4:19).

When you know that God is on your side, then that's really all you need to know, and believe me, you won't care what anyone thinks about you; however, you must always care about what God thinks! I have seen people who were not very good-looking on the outside, but when they were living for God, I could see a glow about them.

When a person has God living on the inside of them, you can recognize the beauty on the inside and the outside of them; they almost look like angels. God certainly is our beautifier, and He's the only One that we should care about what He thinks. And when God calls you out of darkness into His marvelous light, your youth will be renewed like an eagle!

Chapter 11

The Lord Is My Shepherd; I Shall Not Want

In the previous chapter, I told you that my closet was cluttered with clothes. I had so many clothes that I could not fit one more thing in my closet! Well, that pretty much went with everything that I had. I wanted everything and then some! I used to work for a company that sold different varieties of things. The company had several catalogs that people would order from, and let me tell you, these catalogs sold just about everything!

I worked on the phones, and I took orders from people all day long… all day long I was looking at these catalogs! I never could resist a sale, and I bought more junk from these catalogs just because they were on sale! It didn't matter if it was a clothing item, a game that I had no clue how to play, or a weird-looking statue that was seventy percent off! I was obsessed with sales!

If I saw something that I wanted, you better believe that I was determined to get it! Not only that, but the place that I was working at had an outlet store right next door. I would go to that outlet right after work every time that I had the chance! I had to pick up all my orders there, so that did not help me much, "Hmm, let's see what they have on sale." I never thought I had a problem. I thought I was just blessed, blessed, blessed until I realized that I was just one big mess!

One time I remember opening a credit card for this other shopping store so that I could save twenty percent on my purchase. Now just how dumb is that? I really felt like I had a lot of money when I got approved! What to do with all my money but to buy a blue fur mink coat! So I went straight to the coat department, and I tried one on, and I must say that I really liked it! I really wanted it, but I thank God that I had half of mind to make that decision and not get it even with twenty percent off!

I was living in an apartment with my mom, and she wanted me to buy a house for her birthday! My mom always got what she wanted! So I bought a beautiful house, and of course, I needed a lot of stuff to go with my beautiful home. And so, shopping we went! I needed everything new! I needed new furniture! I needed a lot of things to go with our new home because my house was bigger than the apartment that we lived in, and mind you, it was a lot bigger!

I had an upstairs and a downstairs! Can we talk? And I also had very, very big closets to add more clothes! So then, when I would think of something that I wanted for my house, I knew that I had to have it that very minute, and I didn't want to wait either! So I bought so much more stuff that I shouldn't have! Then I opened more credit cards, and well...sad to say, because of it, later down the line, I went bankrupt!

You simply can't buy a new home without buying everything else new...so I thought! I just went to spend like crazy! Once I started doing that, it just never seemed to end! I bought a bunch of junk that I didn't even use! Some of those things that I bought were still in boxes for many years, and I ended up throwing them away! I felt like King Solomon. "And whatsoever my eyes desired, I kept not from them!" (Ecclesiastes 2:10). Ha!

But then my mom got sick, and I couldn't go shopping anymore because I had to stay home with her. We couldn't even go out to eat, and the worst part of it was that I couldn't even go to church! Nothing was about me or about what I wanted anymore! I know to be content is to be happy, and to not want is to be content, but the question is the "how to?" How do I not want? So many times, my flesh would cry out for stuff. It would also cry out for attention!

Then I made a choice to put God first, and when I did that, after a while, I can honestly say that I found myself not wanting anything, and I'm not crying out for things anymore. The famous quote in the Bible that's read at funeral services is found in Psalm 23:1, "The Lord is my Shephard; I shall not want." We know that when we are dead, we certainly won't want anything, so I realize that this scripture is for those who are alive. After all, King David was alive when he wrote it.

I never believed that verse was meant for us who are alive by no means because it just sounds impossible for a person not to want, that is, until I found myself wanting nothing. I realized that the things that I had once desired weren't things that made me happy or complete. And even when I would get what I wanted, I always found myself wanting more! After a while, I realized that all the things that I had desired were not even fulfilling.

People are born wanting things. When kids begin to speak, one of the first words that we tend to hear from them is, "*Mine*!" When we see kids at a grocery store, we will see them grabbing just about anything and everything from the shelf that they can get their hands on! It's really sad to hear so many preachers encouraging people to desire more and to go for the gusto! They say, "Name it, claim it, blab it, and grab it!" And they tell people that God wants us to be blessed, blessed, blessed!

The Bible says that it's God's will that we prosper and be in health, but I'm finding out that we can be prosperous in many ways. A person who has a happy family is rich indeed! When I was younger, I wore a ring on every finger. I wore expensive earrings, watches, bracelets, and necklaces. I have jewelry I don't wear because I don't like wearing it. Now it doesn't do anything for me.

I remember a few years back, when my mom was alive, I went to this place that had a lot of brand-name outlet stores with things from clothing to purses to watches and with great prices. But to my surprise, I didn't care to look for anything for myself. Instead, I found a pair of nice slippers for my mom. I tell my friends not to buy me anything for my birthday and Christmas. They really don't understand that language, and when they buy me something, then I must be polite and say thank you!

The Bible says, "But godliness with contentment is great gain. For we brought nothing into this world, and it is certain we can carry nothing out. And having food and raiment let us be therewith content" (1 Timothy 6:6–8).

What's really funny is when I think about something that I may want for myself, I don't go looking for it like I once used to because now I really do hate shopping! But it never fails that when I go shopping, only because my mom wanted to go, lo and behold, the thing that I have thought about getting for myself ends up right in front of me! What's funnier is that the things that I wanted would always be on sale! I'm talking seventy to eighty percent off!

I know that God would always put the things that I would think about right in front of me because I wasn't even looking for them at the time. The funny thing is that I never even prayed for it, but it was just a thought that I had. Since I started letting go of those desires of wanting anything and everything that wasn't satisfying, then God began to supernaturally supply us with everything that we needed. I didn't have a lot of money, but I had God!

God has been better to me than I could have ever been to myself! Now the only thing that I really desire or want is to be closer to God! He really is more than enough!

Chapter 12

Think on These Things

"Whatsoever things are true, whatsoever things are honest, whatsoever things are just, whatsoever things are pure, whatsoever things are lovely, whatsoever things are of good report; if there be any virtue and if there be any praise, think on these things" (Philippians 4:8).

When I first read this scripture, I really wondered why that verse was put in the Bible! The way things were going in my life, I didn't think that I could think on anything lovely! But one day I experienced a great loss—my refrigerator broke! It was still under warrantee, and so I called the repair man, and he told me that it would be a few days before they could fix it because they needed to order a part.

Meanwhile, I really had to suffer! We may not realize it, but we have many great things that are convenient for us, like a refrigerator. When my refrigerator broke, it was in the middle of winter, and it was freezing cold outside! You couldn't even begin to imagine the stuff I had to go through! I had a spare freezer in the garage that I was able to store the frozen food in.

I also had two Styrofoam ice chests that I kept in the garage so that I could keep the food cold, which included milk, butter, and coffee creamer, along with eggs, mayonnaise, and stuff like that. On top of that, I had to buy ice every other day! My garage was not attached to my house, so I had to go outside in the freezing cold every time that I needed to get something, and I needed to go out a lot!

I must say that was extremely upsetting for me seeing I detest cold weather! I was not a happy camper, and I went to complaining but good! Well, a few days later, they finally fixed my refrigerator, but then, not too long after that, it broke down yet again! I couldn't believe it! But then it hit me, and I was reminded of what I had read in the Bible about how God felt about complainers!

He sure didn't like how much I had been complaining about my refrigerator being broken! When it broke, I never stopped complaining! So the second time that it broke, I knew better than to complain. I remembered Numbers 11 and how the people were complaining so much and how God got really upset! So then after the refrigerator broke the second time, I began to look around at everything else that was a great blessing to me.

And instead of complaining, I began thanking God for other things that I had been blessed with. I thanked Him for my stove that was working, and I thanked Him for my electricity that was working and for the heater that kept me warm after I came back from going outside in the freezing cold to get food from my garage. And when I looked around me, I saw more things to be thankful for.

I was able to see many more blessings that I couldn't see before, and then I was able to think on all these things, things that are lovely. There have been times that God has blessed me silly, but because I had other things on my mind that would stress me out, I was not able to give God the glory that He deserves for His many, many blessings.

When I realized how God had truly blessed me, then I had to ask God to forgive me, and I continued thanking Him for the many blessings that I had. We must be very careful not to let distractions come in and take our mind off our blessings. Just the other day, my microwave broke… Selah…

The Bible says, "Forget not ALL His [God's] benefits" (Psalm 103:2). When a person can truly see the many benefits that God has blessed them with, then they really won't want to stop praising Him! I'm not saying that bad things won't ever happen, but when we can see how the good outweighs the bad, then we can truly think on these things. If you don't think that you have something to be grateful for, then all you need to do is look at the news!

When we can really think on all the wonderful things that God has done for us, then we are truly overcomers! The Bible says, "They overcame by the word of their testimony and by the Blood of Lamb" (Revelation 12:11). We must continue to remind ourselves of the many things that God has done for us and continues to do for us so that we can continue to be overcomers.

One thing that I look at when something bad happens is my health and my family's health; that right there gets me bucking and shouting! When I am hungry, I will think about my empty belly and I will say to myself, *Imagine if I didn't have any food to eat*. And then when I see my hot plate of food... well...I just get to bucking some more!

There are days when it gets extremely hot outside. I imagine not having an air conditioner. Try waking up thinking, *What if I didn't have any soap or toothpaste or even a hairbrush for that matter?* I could go on forever talking about God's many blessings. We truly have so many benefits to think on and thank God for!

It's always good to remember that things can always be worse than they are. The Bible says to take no thought for tomorrow. Not what we should eat or even what we should wear. A major distraction that keeps people from thinking good thoughts is that they are thinking about tomorrow or next week or even next year. Sometimes I still find myself doing that, and when I realize that I am doing that, I repent because we really don't know what tomorrow may bring.

God wants us to have good thoughts because good thoughts bring peace, and He truly gives us so much to be thankful for. "Oh, that men would praise the Lord for his goodness, and for his wonderful works to the children of men! And let them sacrifice the sacrifices of thanksgiving and declare his works with rejoicing" (Psalm 107:21–22). "By Him therefore let us offer sacrifices of praise to God continually, that is the fruit of our lips giving thanks to His Name" (Hebrews 13:15). "Therefore, I will offer in His tabernacle sacrifices of joy; I will sing, yea, I will sing praises unto the Lord" (Psalm 27:6).

I must say that I was shocked when I read these verses! I never heard of praise being a sacrifice, much less joy! So, when we may be facing a trial, it makes it hard for us to see our blessings, and we may not feel like praising God, but when we do it anyway, God considers it to be a sacrifice. In Psalm 116, King David is crying out for his life asking God to rescue him, and yet in verse 17 he is offering the sacrifice of thanksgiving.

I'm not saying that it's an easy thing to do while we are going through something, but one thing I can tell you is that because I have been praising God whether I may have wanted to or not, now it has become automatic for me to do. I know that parents who do so much for their children would love to hear their children thank them for what they do for them. That's got to be such a great feeling! I'm sure that God feels the exact same way when He hears His children thanking Him.

"I will bless the Lord at all times, His praises shall be continually in my mouth!" (Psalm 34:1). God deserves all the praise and all the glory forever. Amen!

Chapter 13

Pride of Life

I often hear so many people today who say that they want so badly to be used by God. Many people have distorted the word *"used"* to the point that people think that to be used is to be famous and to be in lights. The bottom line is if the truth be known that many people just want to be seen and known, and they want the bright light flashing on them! "O *Lord*, please use me!"

I was used one time, and really, it didn't do anything for me but make me think that I was somebody that I was not! Many churches have gotten so far away from the word *"servanthood"* and instead have become a place of so-called Christians who just want plenty of servants serving them! We must really be very careful of that little thing called pride.

Pride is something that slowly creeps in. It will come in when a person has someone carrying their bags for them or when they are offered a seat in the front row with the guest pastors, prophets, evangelists, and whatever else they want to call themselves. I have often had to ask myself if I am being prideful, and I will be honest and tell you that there were many times that I was.

Pride doesn't always appear to look like pride because that spirit is a very sneaky one, and we must really be very careful of that. Even one compliment can do great damage to a person if they are not aware of that spirit. I remember once this hillbilly preacher who was so anointed, and let me tell you that he could preach the house down!

When he preached, the power of God would come down so strong! He would preach with a hillbilly stylish preaching, and he was ever so funny! But then, after a while, I noticed that he wasn't himself anymore. He started learning big influential words instead of using his crazy words that made us laugh hysterically!

Then I noticed that he began to lose his humility and he became arrogant. It seemed like he wanted to be somebody else. What was really sad was that the fire in him began to slowly die, and those words of eloquence that he had learned, well, were just words. I'm not knocking smartness by any means, but I'm just saying don't let smartness take away who you are, lest you don't know anymore!

There have been times in my prayer time that my flesh would rise up, and all kinds of thoughts would enter my mind that just made me mad! This flesh of mine is always wanting, and it's also thinking that I am better than other people, and it is ever so selfish! When I started writing this book, my flesh would get to talking away! My flesh would tell me stuff like, "When I finish this book, I will be popular and great!" Woo-hoo!

There were many times that I would find myself struggling with thinking something great could happen for *meeee*! But as I began to read the Bible, I could see where greatness really lies. It's certainly not in earthly possessions or high positions, but real freedom comes when we become God's servants and serve. When my mind would continually run wildly telling me how great I was, I just had to remind my mind of who I really was!

Without God I'm just a dingy, dumb, and confused girl who doesn't know her right hand from her left! True story! Please don't ever tell me to raise my right hand! I needed to shine the bright light of the Word of God in my face in order to see that pride of mine!

For some reason people tend to forget where it is they came from, or shall I say where God has brought them from. And so we can get big-headed really over nothing…just wait till the hair starts turning white and the teeth start decaying…well, must I go on? I am not great, nor do I want to be! There is only One who is great, and that is God Almighty!

We see what happens to so many so-called great people! I remember when I heard this famous actor who was being interviewed once say that he wanted to jump out of a window, and he said that he didn't know why. This person has it all, so why in the world would he think that way? We can see how the rich and famous are committing suicide and many who have overdosed on something.

Do we really want to be great? We really have to selah about that. My flesh wants to make it big! My flesh wants to be seen! My flesh wants to be noticed, but the problem is I don't want any of those things because I have put my spirit before my flesh. As I allow my spirit man to rule, then God shows me what really is good!

When I first got saved, I told God that I just wanted to have peace, joy, and happiness. If anyone has those things, they need to realize that they are truly blessed! You can't put a price tag on that; that is something that the world can't give you. God is the only One who can give us real joy and peace, and I can honestly say that there ain't nothing fake about that; it's the real McCoy!

When we see who we really are compared to God and His greatness, then we will be able to see how much of a nothing we really are. It's only when we truly see God that we can truly see ourselves. God is light, and we just can't help seeing ourselves when His light is shining brightly. That is why it's hard for so many to read the Bible!

One time I made a huge mistake! I went to this store that had all kinds of cool stuff to buy. It was one of my favorite stores because they had massage chairs in their store, and my mom and I loved to sit on them! So, as I was roaming around looking at things, I saw this cool makeup mirror with lights, and on the back of the mirror was a magnifying mirror; most women know what I am talking about. But this was a really cool-looking one, and it stood out.

So I went to look at it, and then I turned it around to the side to the magnifying mirror, and then I turned on the lights, and they were ever so bright! When I looked at the mirror with the bright lights on, I went into total shock! This was years ago, and I was not as old as I am now. At the time, I was still looking good. So, when I looked closely in the mirror with those bright lights, I just freaked out at what I saw! It was really gross!

I must say that was quite a humbling experience for me! The deep calleth! Ha! I never want to do that again! When we read the Bible, there will be a very bright light shining on us, and that light is only to show us what needs to be fixed on the inside of us. What I saw when I started reading the Bible was very gross!

I often think of some people who once were once in the limelight but got prideful and fell. I don't think about them to belittle them, but I think about them to remind myself of what pride does to a person. The Bible says, "Pride goeth before destruction and a haughty spirit before a fall" (Proverbs 16:18). If a person becomes prideful, we must understand that it won't be very long before they fall!

Pride can also creep up on us when we accomplish great things or become well-known. It will also creep up on us when we are not well-known, but we may hang around someone who is! Look at meeee! Pride is no respecter of persons! God really hates pride! Think of it: He cast Lucifer out of heaven because of his pride, and He created a really bad place for him and for the angels that followed him called hell.

Hell was never meant for us, but when we follow Satan, we are following him all the way there. We can also read in the New Testament and see that God hates pride so much that He even turns people over to a reprobate mind, meaning they don't have their right mind, and they have no clue that they don't.

> *Because that, when they knew God, they glorified him not as God, neither were thankful; but became vain in their imaginations, and their foolish heart was darkened. Professing themselves to be wise, they became fools, And even as they did not like to retain God in their knowledge, God gave them over to a reprobate mind, to do those things which are not convenient.*
>
> Romans 1:21–22, 28

Do you know someone who is always thinking that they are right, and yet everybody just knows differently? Pride doesn't show up at the door in an ugly form, but it paints a beautiful picture of "*self*," and it slowly creeps in! "Ye shall be as gods" (Genesis 3:5). Pride can begin with a compliment from someone who will tell you something that makes you feel good.

It's okay to occasionally receive a compliment, but it's far better not to have too many lest it gets to our head and then our heart. Humility is the key that will save your soul! I try to always remember my past of where God brought me from so that I can cast my wicked, wicked, prideful thoughts out of my head!

We want a title; we want the lights, the microphones, and the stage, but we must remember that when we are on the stage, people will see the good, the bad, and the ugly! And when the lights are shining brightly, you can be sure that all your flaws will be seen!

I remember when some friends at church told me that she and her father wanted to volunteer. She told me that the workers in charge of the volunteers were very rude, and they had to stop volunteering because of that; these people were just the sweetest and kindest people. If a pastor is wondering why they can't get volunteers, then maybe they should check their staff!

"But whoso shall offend one of these little ones which believe in me, it were better for him that a millstone were hanged about his neck, and that he were drowned in the depth of the sea" (Matthew 18:6).

Every church should have somewhere where their congregation or their sheep can give a report about how their leaders are treating them whether good or bad. They should put a person of character who walks after the Spirit to read them. If they do that, I'm sure you will see a wave of humility in your staff!

Pastors need to realize that the devils come to church disguising themselves in light and are given a badge to wear, and they are there to devour your sheep! It's time to get your flashlights out, and if you see or even hear about a leader in your church mistreating your sheep and misrepresenting God, then you need to start rebuking, reproving, and correcting them lest their blood and the blood of bleeding sheep will be on your hands!

Stop putting people on high pedal stools! That's not biblical, and you are sending those people straight to hell! "Well, I don't want to hurt nobody's feeling; after all they are so faithful." "They're always there for me." All I can say is if you don't have a spine and don't care about how God feels, then get off the sacred pulpit of God and get saved!

When a pastor allows prideful leaders to lead in their church, they are not only allowing them to mistreat the sheep, but they are also allowing those leaders to raise other church members to become like them! A leader will always get followers! "Woe unto you, scribes and Pharisees, hypocrites! for ye compass sea and land to make one proselyte, and when he is made, ye make him twofold more the child of hell than yourselves" (Matthew 23:15).

"For the time is come that judgment must begin at the house of God: and if it first begin at us, what shall the end be of them that obey not the gospel of God?" (1 Peter 4:17).

If you have cold Christians who are leaders in your church, then you really can't expect to see a move of God! It's time for church leaders to start igniting the flames of the fire of God by bearing the fruit of humility and having compassion for the people if you truly want to see souls saved! The devil knows that his time is short, and we need to be ready for the battlefield! People are going to hell each and every day!

There is no time for babying leaders who want all the attention on themselves! We need grown-up leaders who know how to fight devils by seeking God, praying, and fasting; instead, we have a bunch of leaders who are whining about getting a higher position! "Woe is me!" We are not supposed to be working unto man, but we are supposed to be working for God and God alone!

I'm really not trying to preach here, but I have seen so many people become prideful just because they may do something for someone important, and I watched the explosion of pride set in, and it so sickens me! I can see why God hates pride! People may not realize it, but pride will not only make you roll your eyes in the back of your head, but it will leave you with a bad odor!

I urge people to please beware of that spirit! If Lucifer was able to turn a third of God's glorious angels against God and convince them to leave God and heaven and he convinced Eve to go against God, then who are we? The Bible tells us to be vigilant for a reason. "Be sober, be vigilant; because your adversary the devil, as a roaring lion, walketh about, seeking whom he may devour" (1 Peter 5:8).

> *The transgression of the wicked saith within my heart, that there is no fear of God before his eyes. For he flattereth himself in his own eyes, until his iniquity be found to be hateful. The*

words of his mouth are iniquity and deceit: he hath left off to be wise, and to do good.

He deviseth mischief upon his bed; he setteth himself in a way that is not good; he abhorreth not evil. How excellent is thy lovingkindness, O God! therefore the children of men put their trust under the shadow of thy wings. For with thee is the fountain of life: in thy light shall we see light.

O continue thy lovingkindness unto them that know thee; and thy righteousness to the upright in heart. Let not the foot of pride come against me, and let not the hand of the wicked remove me. There are the workers of iniquity fallen: they are cast down, and shall not be able to rise.

Psalm 36:1–4, 7, 9–12

If my people who are called by my name shall humble themselves and pray...then...I will!

Chapter 14

Casting Down Imaginations

(For the weapons of our warfare are not carnal, but mighty through God to the pulling down of strong holds;) Casting down imaginations, and every high thing that exalteth itself against the knowledge of God, and bringing into captivity every thought to the obedience of Christ.

2 Corinthians 10:4–5

The mind is a terrible thing to waste! When a person did or said something that made me feel bad, I would always try to figure out why they did what they did or said what they said, but I realized that I was wasting my time and my mind by doing that. I realized that whatever thought that I allowed to stay in my mind would end up controlling me. We're like the great big ship that is turned by a very small helm as we ourselves are led by very small thoughts.

The Bible talks about the tongue being out of control, but I'm finding out that our thoughts can get out of control as well. Even though we may not realize it, a text message or a Facebook comment and even a tweet can totally control our mind, emotions, our days, and even our lives depending on what we do with those thoughts.

Far too many people spend too much time looking at their phone, computer, and Facebook. "Did someone text me?" "Did someone Facebook me?" "Did anyone like me?" "Did someone see my face?" "Is anybody looking, listening, or paying attention to me?" I think people put themselves out there just to get attention from anyone, and while they are sitting there waiting and wondering if they are, the clock is ticking away!

All this stuff comes into our minds only to distract us. If we're not careful, it will keep our minds wandering in la-la land! It will also keep us from having a life, for that matter! "Mom, you've been on that thing all day!" "Mom, the baby's hungry." "Hold on, I need to see if I'm important!" And those thoughts can keep a person from getting closer to their loved ones and to God.

When I start praying, distractions will be sure to come—my phone may ring, or my dogs may want attention. Sometimes my stomach will start growling, and all of a sudden, I'm starving to death! There were many times that I just couldn't seem to focus on praying, and everything would become one big blur! If we want to get alone time with God, we must put the phone away, and if we don't do that, we may lose that time that we have taken to spend with God.

We may get a text from someone, and that one text can end up taking all the time that we need to spend with God as we continue to text away. There have been many times when I was at church listening to the pastor preach, and then these stupid thoughts would come to my mind, and those thoughts would make me miss some of the message that the pastor was preaching on. I would get so upset because I couldn't pay attention to preaching because of my thoughts!

I really hate it when my thoughts make me lose my concentration! I can be watching a movie, and all of a sudden, another movie will be playing in my head. Maybe not an actual movie, but a whole bunch of thoughts will be playing! We have to understand that unless we learn how to eliminate our thoughts, they will not leave, and that's one of the reasons why it's so hard for people to pray and read the Bible.

I must admit that there were many times when I went and prayed, and I would end up thinking about so many things; then by the time I knew it, I had spent an hour sitting on the floor doing nothing but thinking dumb thoughts! We may spend time looking at the clock twenty-five times while we are trying to pray. We may be thinking about what we have to do for that day! Why?

I realized that for a person to fight thoughts is as hard as someone fighting someone in a wrestling match! Thoughts are very hard to fight, and they can be very big in our mind. I found out that one way to fight thoughts is to replace them with other thoughts. In other words, we need to replace our mind with Jesus's mind.

The Bible says, "Let this mind be in you which was also in Christ Jesus" (Philippians 2:5). It also says for us to be transformed by the renewing of our mind. "And be not conformed to this world: but be ye transformed by the renewing of your mind, that ye may prove what is that good, and acceptable, and perfect, will of God" (Romans 12:2).

Sounds simple enough, but I must say that the "how to" is not easy! Even though I've had a lot of practice, and I am getting so much better at casting my thoughts down, there are times that I still face battles of having to really fight off certain thoughts. The first thoughts that I had to start fighting off were the thoughts of me thinking that I knew what was going to happen and what I assumed what God was going to do.

I remember the many times that I would spend trying to think of ways to make things happen the way that I felt that things should happen, or shall I say the way that I wanted God to make things happen. I would spend hours upon hours doing this! I was obsessed until I learned more about who God was. When I read the verses that said God would do whatever He pleased (Psalm 135:6, 115:3), then I knew that my way of thinking was not going to change a doggone thing!

When I carry so many thoughts in my mind, it feels like I'm carrying a bunch of weight in my head, and I must say, they can get quite heavy! Your mind can be on your marriage, your kids, your bills, and the list goes on! The thoughts of my mom and my dogs alone used to be quite a heavy-duty weight on me! And when they got sick, it felt like a bomb just exploded in my face!

We may all face challenges on a daily basis, and many thoughts will come with those challenges. The question is, do those thoughts keep you from enjoying the many things that God provides for you?

Do your dogs constantly irritate you when they bark? Do you appreciate the hot plate of food that God has blessed you with? Where is your focus? Are the thoughts of the doctor's appointment that's two weeks away distracting you? How about your children's future or their safety? How about your job? What thoughts are keeping you from receiving God's peace?

Not too long ago, I couldn't help looking at my cell phone for calls. When my mom was alive, I didn't talk on the phone, nor did I like to. I was always busy taking care of her, and I wanted to spend my free time with her and my dogs. So my phone hardly ever rang. But for some reason I couldn't stop picking up my cell phone every fifteen minutes and looking at it to see if anyone had called.

I wasn't expecting anyone to call, but I just couldn't help looking at it to see if someone called. Then it started up with the computer. I had never gotten emails, but for some reason I was constantly looking at my computer for emails. That was just crazy! It was like something was controlling me and making me do this!

That got me so mad because it was taking time away from me! Then I remembered the verse, "Whatsoever ye shall bind on earth shall be bound in heaven" (Matthew 18:18), and I began yelling out, "I bind you, devil!" And right after I said those words a few times, then the urge to look at the phone or the computer left! God's Word is powerful!

Another battle with my thoughts that I was fighting was when people told me that they needed help or that they were having a hard time with something. When I tried to help them, they would refuse my help. It was hard for me to let go because I really wanted to help them only because I knew that I could, and I would have a really hard time forgetting about it, and I would waste so much time wondering why they wouldn't let me help them make their life so much easier. Maybe people just want to rant! Go on Facebook and leave me alone!

Casting down imaginations and even strongholds takes a lot of work! But after I began using God's Word to fight against and to conquer those miserable thoughts, then my mind became clear again. It was so crazy because after casting down so many thoughts from my mind, then I didn't even know what to think about! My mind was actually empty! It kind of felt weird!

I didn't have bills on my mind anymore, I didn't have "Is my mom getting sick?" on my mind, and those tormenting thoughts of "What if my dogs get sick?" even left my mind. I didn't realize how much garbage was on my mind, but it was overflowing all right! Now all I think about is God and His goodness! Is it possible? Yes, and it feels so good to be free! Ask yourself if your thoughts are full of fear or faith, worries or blessings.

Now I can sit outside on my swing and enjoy the gentle breeze outside, and I can watch the beautiful sunset with amazement! Now I can listen to the birds chirping away and can look with admiration at how God has created everything so perfectly. When God created everything, it was for His pleasure, and He also created everything for us to enjoy.

The reason that we can't even enjoy anything that God created for us to enjoy is simply because our mind won't let us! Is it possible for us to enjoy life as bad as things are going these days? That all depends on what we are allowing our minds to think. Are you afraid wondering if the man who just moved in next door to you is a psychopath? Or are you putting your trust in God and believing that He is big enough to keep you from all evil and that He will protect you from harm's way?

When we truly believe that we have the power that God says that we have, then we can take authority over any unwanted thoughts. As I stated earlier about the tormenting thoughts over my non-cellulite legs, I believe that many people may be facing tormenting thoughts about their looks. They can be tormented over the way their eyes look or the way that their hair looks. I can say now that I'm older, I have cellulite, and I really don't care!

I started reading this book called *The Broken Mirror*. The author is Katharine A. Philips, MD. It talks about people with body dysmorphic disorders. The people in her book believe that they are ugly when they are not. These people focus on a part of their body, whether it's their hair or nose or body, and believe that what they are focusing on is ugly.

I could relate to this book because when I was really young, I felt like I had a big nose, and I would always look at my nose in the mirror. What I was doing was magnifying my nose just like I was magnifying my non-cellulite legs, and those thoughts would just get bigger in my mind.

I thank God that my problem was not nearly as severe as the people in the book and that it was just a phase that I went through. This book was truly an eye-opener for me. I'm older now, and I don't look like I used to when I was younger, but God's really not worried about the outer appearance, so why should I be?

Now when I look in the mirror, the only thing that I worry about is what I see in the inward part, and if something does not look right, then you better believe that I'm going to be thinking about that and how to fix it up! You can be sure that I will be on my knees asking for God to help me make it look right so that I can look all pretty on the inside for my Jesus!

Every day in my prayer time, I quote the verse in the beginning of this chapter, casting down all my imaginations, and I cast all my cares upon God. Then I tell God, "I'm here for You." I will say that by doing that day by day, my thoughts decrease, and His thoughts have increased! I will say that it did not happen overnight, but nevertheless, it happened! God's Word really works!

Chapter 15

Seek First the Kingdom of God

"But seek ye first the kingdom of God, and his righteousness; and all these things shall be added unto you"

Matthew 6:33

When I began seeking God and spending time with Him was when God began to show me the things that I have written. I wouldn't have known about my stupid thinking unless I had been seeking God. But I had to choose to take the time that I needed to spend in prayer and in His Word so God could show me these things. God has so many things to tell us if we just put Him first.

I was reading the Bible in 1 Chronicles 13, which talks about King David bringing the ark of God into the city of David. When I read this, I was really shocked because this day was supposed to be a glorious day for the Israelites! The people were so happy, and they were singing and dancing as they were bringing the ark of God, but God was not happy, and He killed a man during this celebration.

At first, I didn't understand why this happened. I had read this part of the Bible many times until God opened my eyes. What happened was when King David decided to bring the ark to the city of David, he didn't go to God about it first, but instead, he asked the people what they had thought about bringing the ark back, and all the people agreed that it was the right thing to do.

So they placed the ark of God in a new cart, and when they were bringing it, the Bible says, "And David and all Israel played before God with all their might, and with singing, and with harps, and with psalteries, and with timbrels, and with cymbals, and with trumpets" (1 Chronicles 13:8). It wasn't a bad thing that he wanted to do, and actually it was a very good thing to do.

But since King David didn't go to God first and do things in order, then God got really upset, and He killed Uzza…yes, God killed a man. People who don't believe that God kills people are just very uninformed, or they may be in denial! But it's all there in the Bible! Even though Uzza's intentions were very good, and he was just trying to keep the ark from falling to the ground, because things were not done in God's order, then Uzza was killed.

And what's even crazier was that all the people were praising God at the time that God killed Uzza! King David knew why God got mad, and he said that none should carry the ark but the Levites (1 Chronicles 15:2). God killed Uzza because King David had placed the wrong people to stand by the ark of God.

I was so confused about this passage until I kept reading, and I had to read till I got to the fifteenth chapter in order to see the reason for poor Uzza's death. This is why it is so important to hear from God and not just listen to the leaders. We must understand that leaders mess up! I thank God for people who write books under the inspiration of the Holy Spirit because I actually found God through reading someone's book.

I really didn't know God because for us to really know God takes continual seeking His Word, and there's just no going around that. Do you want to be a doctor, a lawyer, an architect? Then you must seek. You must read many books and study very, very hard! The more that I have learned about God, the more I began to hunger and thirst for more of Him.

I can truly say that through my seeking God, I was able to find the One True God, the love of my life, the everlasting Father, the keeper of my soul! People may feel like they know God because they may have experienced His presence here and there. They may have also experienced His blessings, and that may seem to be all that they really know about God.

Even though those things are great to experience, I'm finding out that there is so much more to experience in God than what we could ever expect—

deep and wide! God's Word says that we go from glory to glory—the more you grow, the more you will glow! When we don't go to God and put Him first in our lives is like a person trying to drive a car without putting gas in it. You will get nowhere!

People can be really busy and always be on the go, but if they don't go to God first for direction, they will find themselves in the same spot that they started out at, and they simply will not get ahead. God has all the answers that we need. Sometimes God will only give us the answer that we need for the day, and that's only because He wants us to seek Him on a daily basis for everything that we may need each and every day.

As time flies so fast these days, I know that it's not easy to find the time that we need to spend with God. We have places to go and people to see and people to feed, and don't forget about shopping for sales! But when something bad happens, like we get sick or maybe our car breaks down in the middle of the road, then we don't have a choice but to wait and wait and wait until we get better or we get the help that we need.

It was when bad things started happening in my life that all of a sudden, I had all the time in the world to get with my Jesus, and I'm so ashamed to say that it was not by choice either. Not too long ago, I heard about a married couple whose husband had just retired. They had all kinds of stuff planned for their retirement, and they had plenty of money saved up.

One day they were driving down the road, and someone hit their car. The person who hit them was texting on their phone instead of watching where they were going. The husband was okay, but the wife was not. She was in a coma for quite a while. The husband was with her at the hospital every day until she passed.

We can sit and wait two hours at an amusement park in order to get on one ride that lasts about a minute, and we will wait in the heat of the day for that one-minute ride! We can sit at a doctor's office for forty-five minutes to an hour and a half with no distractions whatsoever, but then when it comes to giving our Creator time—the One who created us—then we just can't seem to make time to spend with Him. Technology can be a wonderful thing!

When I'm driving in my car, I don't sit there and think. I don't listen to the radio, but I've got my Bible CD playing. Many people waste time sitting and waiting and wondering and hoping day by day for something good to happen in their lives. I'm here to say that as much as I waited and wondered and hoped for something good to happen, nothing ever changed.

I'm not talking about waiting for a change in a career or moving to another place, but I'm talking about a spiritual change. Nothing will change in a person's life one doggone bit unless a person decides to change their schedule around for God and give Him the time that He needs so that He can lead them in the direction that they need to go. I got to the point that I was tired of waiting and wondering and hoping that things would just change all by themselves!

I had a good life, but there was a hole in my life that needed filling, and I didn't want to go one more day living the way that I was. So, when I gave God all my attention, I realized that I didn't have to sit there and wonder and hope and wait anymore, but now I can just know! As I read the Bible, I'm learning more about the God of Abraham, Isaac, and Jacob.

I'm also learning what God is capable of, and there are even times that God lets me know why He allows and disallows certain things in my life. Now I am confident that God is leading me wherever He wants me to go. I understand that His ways are much higher than mine! I know that He will completely heal my heart and that things will get better!

Now I know why I suffer, and I know why I hurt. And even if I don't know His exact plans for me, I can say that when you know the Maker, then you can be at peace while you allow Him to take you through this thing called *life*! I love it because I don't even care what God's plans are for me. I really don't!

As long as I know that God is leading the way, I don't need to think about where I am going. I'm just going along for the ride! I really don't need to worry or even think about my future when God is leading my life. And the really great thing about this is that this life here on earth won't last always!

I know there's a far better life waiting for me, and the end results will only bring forth new beginnings! I will be with my King of kings and Lord of lords forever and ever and ever! The Bible tells us that if we draw nigh to God, He will draw nigh to us, but if we don't...que será, será...

Chapter 16

God's Ways Are Higher

"For my thoughts are not your thoughts, neither are your ways my ways, saith the Lord. For as the heavens are higher than the earth, so are my ways higher than your ways, and my thoughts than your thoughts"

Isaiah 55:8–9

One thing I've learned is that when I want things to go the way that they should go, only because it just seems to make so much sense to me, they don't! As I stated earlier, things usually never go the way that I think they should go. I realize that's because God's ways are so much higher than mine! So now I stop trying to think how things will go altogether, and I get to casting down those thoughts of mine!

Sometimes when God shows me things, I really get frantic! When God would give me dreams of things that could happen to someone, guess what I thought? I thought that I was the savior, and I would try to help God fix things. When we get to the point that God shows us things, we really must be careful. Sometimes God will tell us stuff that will happen, but that doesn't mean that it will happen right away. It may not even happen till a hundred years later.

So we really shouldn't get so excited when God shows us something to the point that we try to help God out, that is, unless God specifically tells us to do so. For example, what if the people in the Old Testament started looking for the virgin who was supposed to give birth to our Savior? That would have been a total mess! "We want our Savior now; bless God!" "Gather all the virgins together!"

When Jesus came to this planet, people tried to make Him a King. People just get to thinking way too much! I must admit that when I had my say about things versus God's say, I just ended up making things worse, and I could hear God laughing at me because of it! I used to have this magnet on my refrigerator that said, "We plan, God laughs!" This is so true indeed!

What's really funny is that sometimes when God tells me stuff, then I automatically think that I am smart! Just how dumb is that? God just told me something that I didn't know! We are born with this "I am so smart" mentality, and we feel that way just because we figured something out, and then we get bigheaded and feel like we can conquer the world all by ourselves!

Though men and women may be wise enough to do certain things like build and create great things, when it comes to having a good relationship with their spouse or children, then they have no clue how to make things work. Hmm. Let's not forget that God gave us our mind to think, and He sure 'nuff can take it away at any given moment!

I realize that men and women do not have all the answers, but they just have the desire to have all the answers, and sadly many of them have a really hard time admitting that they don't. Too often people run around looking for someone who they believe will have the answers that they need; been there, done that! I have spent a lot of time trying to think of a person that I could go to for answers.

I just wanted to talk to someone so that I could get answers to certain questions that I had. I guess I just wanted someone to be there for me to help lead me in the right direction. God removed everyone out of my life who I thought could help me so that there was no one to go to but Him. I found out that only God has all the answers, and as we seek Him first, we can be sure that He doesn't mind sharing them with us!

Remember His Word says, "Call unto me and I will answer thee" (Jeremiah 33:3). God will give us the answer that we need, but we must be patient and wait for them. We must be willing to listen and follow His instructions if we want to hear Him, and we definitely must give up trying to figure things out ourselves. There have been times that God has told me things that didn't even make sense to my natural mind, but He assured me that it was Him talking.

Unless you know that you know that you know that God is talking, you will be very confused trying to figure out if God is really talking or not. The Bible says, "God is not the author of confusion, but the God of peace" (1 Corinthians 14:33). So I strongly suggest if you are not positively sure that God is talking to you, then just wait until you know without a shadow of a doubt and let peace have her perfect work.

One way for a person to know that God is talking is for them to know His Word. The Bible says, "It is the spirit that quickeneth; the flesh profiteth nothing: the WORDS that I speak unto you, they are spirit, and they are life" (John 6:63). And since He is His Word and His Word is Spirit, then we must live by His Word in order to receive the answers that we need from God.

When we have God's Word in us, then we have Him in us. "If ye abide in me, and my words abide in you, ye shall ask what ye will, and it shall be done unto you" (John 15:7). God speaks through His Word. There have been times when God would tell me to do something, and I was not sure it was Him, and He would confirm it with His Word.

I have questioned God many times when He would tell me something, and that's because my way of thinking just seemed so right, and God's ways seemed way out there! But I learned that God really doesn't need our mind, and He sure doesn't need our counsel! Once you really get to know God, after a while, you will realize that your own opinions just don't matter!

Just take a moment and think of where your mind has gotten you thus far! Peace, peace, wonderful peace... Have you felt like you were a hamster in a wheel going around in circles and ending up nowhere? When you allow God to direct your life, He will take you where He wants you to go, and He will lead you to do what He wants you to do, and you will know that it is Him, no questions asked.

Even though I have been led by God to do what He wants me to do and go where He wants me to go, sometimes I still find myself questioning what to do next because I feel like I should be doing something for God, but I realize that when I do that, I allow confusion to set in, and I lose my peace. I really don't want to go on my own way of thinking anymore.

God is not confused, and He will close doors that need to be closed and open doors that need to be opened. There are times that I feel like I'm wasting my life by not thinking and by not doing things that I feel that I should be doing. The Bible says, "They that wait upon the Lord shall renew their strength" (Isaiah 40:31).

When I take time and think about what I think of what should happen or what I should be doing, I find myself feeling drained, and I start feeling pressure in my mind, but when I give everything over to God, He just takes over! I'm not saying it's easy, but I'm saying when you allow God to control your life, He will lead you and direct your steps.

When I think about all the dumb things that I have done in my life, I realize that it's because I wasn't thinking straight, or shall I say that "my" mind was doing all the thinking! Now I know that my mind is good for nothing! Have you ever thrown away something that you really shouldn't have?

Or maybe you waited too long to do something that you know that you should have done, and because you waited, you missed out on something very important. How many times have you misplaced your keys, your shoes, or your glasses? That's how puny our minds are! "Heavenly Father, please tell me the direction to my car keys!"

Every morning that I wake up, I cry out to God for His help because I realize how really dumb I am on my own. When I look at the news and see all the chaos and dilemma that's taking place today, and I see everyone looking like they're walking around with no head wondering what in the world they are going to do in order to fix things, then I realize just how dumb everybody is!

Not making fun of anyone, but just realizing what man really is. When you begin to see just how smart God is and compare Him to man's smartness, you will begin to really appreciate being around Him. Before Adam and Eve ate the fruit, we had one hundred percent use of our brain function, but after they ate the fruit, it seems like we lost just about ninety-seven percent! Don't believe me; just look at the many broken relationships today!

If just two people can't figure out how to get along in a relationship, then what happens when more people are added…friends, kids, *in-laws*…? I heard that we may use eight percent of our minds, but that's for the very smart people! So here we are with three percent use of our brain trying to figure out God's ways.

If you are tired of living a stressful life, then let God lead. The Bible says, "Casting all your cares upon Him; for He careth for you" (1 Peter 5:7), so why in the world would you want to hang on to them? All you have to do is give God your keys and take His keys, which is the Word of Life, and let Him take you where you are supposed to go and relax!

Chapter 17

Without Faith It's Impossible

"For God so loved the world, that he gave his only begotten Son, that whosoever believeth in him should not perish, but have everlasting life"

John 3:16

Sadly, this scripture has been so misinterpreted in saying that God loves the world, and that's it—people feel that they can live in any way that they want to. When I began to study the Bible, I realized that there was so much more to this verse. When I read the part that says, "Whosoever believeth in him should not perish but have everlasting life," then I realized that God was offering everlasting life to those who believe in Him.

The Bible says, "He that believeth on him is not condemned: but he that believeth not is condemned already, because he hath not believed in the name of the only begotten Son of God" (John 3:18). It also says, "He that believeth and is baptized shall be saved; but he that believeth not shall be damned" (Mark 16:16). Now that's a pretty rough statement; nevertheless, it's God's Word. Keep in mind that Jesus is the One who spoke those words.

"But without faith it is impossible to please him: for he that cometh to God must believe that he is, and that He is a rewarder of them that diligently seek him" (Hebrews 11:6). This scripture is saying that if we don't have faith, then we don't believe in Him, and therefore, we cannot even be pleasing to God. While I was going through my trials, I realized that I didn't have faith in God.

I wanted to, and I even believed I did, but when things would get bad for me, then I would always find myself stressing out. That was when I realized that I didn't really believe. I know that Romans 12:3 says that God gives us a measure of faith, but I have to say that my faith was not really noticeable at all! I can also say that while I was going through my trials, my faith began increasing, and for that, I am ever grateful!

Sadly, today many Christians really believe that they have faith in God, but I have learned that when a person goes through a testing period is when they will learn what kind of faith they really have. One easy way for a person to test their faith is when they get sick.

I don't know about anyone else, but when I got sick, I used to always think the worst! "I can't stop coughing; I'm going to die!" And when my mom sniffles, forgeeet about eeet! Panic, panic, panic! I honestly felt like I was the most faithless person in the entire world! So when trials came, I was able to see how much faith I didn't have! I was a total wimp!

I can't believe how I would freak out at anything and everything! I'm finding out that God doesn't give us tasks that we can pass with flying colors. A heavyweight champion doesn't look for someone to fight that he knows that he can defeat, but he looks for the undefeated! It looks like God seems to work the same way too!

When a person picks on someone smaller than themselves to fight, then that's not really a fight. So, when God wants to build our faith in Him...let's just say He won't put millions of dollars in your bank account and ask you to trust Him for a car payment! Just for a person to believe in the invisible God is really a fight indeed!

When I started going through my trials, I had to decide what I was going to do. I wanted to get drunk so that I wouldn't have to think about it because what happened to me just didn't make an ounce of sense! As I said earlier, I felt like I was in the twilight zone! The craziest things were happening...kind of like what's happening in the world today!

We can see that everything is certainly upside down! I couldn't believe what was happening, and I went into a state of shock! It was very devastating for me because I didn't see it coming. I thank God that through it all, my faith rose up! It took years for me to finally heal; it also took years for my faith to increase as much as it did.

I'm finding out that faith doesn't just increase by itself, but faith comes through tests and trials. It didn't take me going through one trial to get the faith that I now have, but it took going through many. As I went through each trial, it was like I was taking one step of faith, and mind you, my steps were baby steps!

I began realizing that my faith was not in God, but my faith was in man. I believed in preachers! When it came to the real test of faith, I must say that I flunked miserably! God had to get me alone in order to get me to call upon Him and only Him. He removed all my contacts so that I couldn't call on anyone but Him!

I can honestly say that each step of faith that I took brought me closer to God. I must admit that I didn't feel close to God after the first few steps, but I had to take many steps in order for my faith in Him to really flourish; that was when I began to feel closer to Him. I had to face many trials in order to get where I am today.

I know my faith in God is very strong, and I am happy to say that I am at the place that I know that I know that I know that God is in control of my life! I don't want to follow any one person, but I only want to follow God! I am at the point that if something doesn't happen, then it simply wasn't meant to happen.

Now, I don't try and make things happen, no matter how bad I may want them to. I simply do my part, and if things don't work out the way that I'd like them to, then I know that it wasn't part of God's plan. I never want to go ahead of God. I'd much rather stay behind Him, and as long as He's leading, I'm okay with whatever happens.

I can say that I have been walking in blind faith. I literally feel like I have blindfolds on because I really don't look ahead. I dare not try to walk out this thing called life on my own, lest I end up falling into a trap! I was reading through the book of Numbers, and it talks about when God's cloud rested on the tabernacle, then the people rested, and when the cloud moved, then the people moved (Numbers 6:17–23).

I know when that cloud is moving, and I know when it's resting because God just lets me know. I may not know where it's going, but I know that as long as I follow it, then I'm going in the right direction. God's ways are perfect, and even though things may not look so good, I know that no matter what, all things are working together for my good because I so love *him*! (Romans 8:28).

I learned that God will always have tests for us. There have been times I felt my faith wavering as other tests came. Unfortunately, we are still human beings that get tired and weary. There have been times when I would get very busy, and it was hard for me to set time away for God like I'm used to doing.

A while back I was moving to a different state, and there was so much that needed to be done. I noticed that my faith started going down, and my fears began taking over. So I had to make that decision to make time for God no matter if I had to get up earlier than usual. And when I did that, immediately I could feel my faith rise.

We really don't want to go anywhere without putting on our shield of faith. All the devil needs is to be able to hit us with those fiery darts when we are off guard, and I must say that those fiery darts are not only painful, but they will make you fear! Faith is simply knowing God! As I read the Bible through each year, then I begin to see more of who God is.

Every time that I read about what God did, I am filled with amazement! God is great and when you read just how great He is, then you begin to understand His greatness. It's kind of like when a child has a father who is famous. I'm sure that child is proud of their father when they see him on television and watch how the people admire and respect him.

So, when I read about God, I feel so proud of Him and all His greatness! I love reading about Him fighting for Israel and how He defeats their enemies without Israel even being present! It's unexplainable how I feel because it's just such an awesome feeling! And that's just one part of God!

There is just so much to learn about God. You will learn of His mercy and His love, His goodness and His justice. I could sit here and write about all that I have learned about who God is, and it would take many pages, but thank God that Book has already been written and made available for all to read!

Another great thing about reading the Bible is that you are filling yourself with His seed, and you can be sure that it will grow! When you truly believe in God and who He is, then your faith will quench all the devil's fiery darts! "Above all, taking the shield of faith, wherewith ye shall be able to quench all the fiery darts of the wicked" (Ephesians 6:16).

When we have faith, we will know that without a shadow of a doubt, God is for us and that absolutely nothing can come against us...*period*! *Only believe*!

Chapter 18

Love Your Neighbor as Yourself

Lately, I have been going outside more and talking to people who are not saved. I can tell you that they are real people with real problems. A new neighbor just moved in next door to me. I have just met her the other day, and we had a good conversation. The neighbors who had lived there before them were quite distant. My new neighbor is a mother of two young boys. I introduced myself to her while she was moving in, and I warned her about my sassy dogs!

She seemed a little distant at first, and I had to respect that. My dogs didn't help any by being unfriendly and all, but I really wanted things to be different with my new neighbors. There were bad things that started happening in our neighborhood, and so I told her what to watch for. She was really concerned about her children because she told me that the place where she used to live had gotten robbed twice.

She told me that she didn't allow her sons to be outside because she was afraid that something bad would happen to them. I let her know that I worked from home and that I would keep a watch out for her house and her children, and I let her know if she ever needed anything, she could ask me. Since she just moved in, she didn't know what days to take the trash out. It changed every holiday, so instead of telling her the dates, I would just take her garbage out for her, and when she saw me do that, she was in shock!

One day I came home from going to the store, and I saw her kids outside. It was raining out, and it looked like a storm was heading our way. The boys told me that they had lost their house keys. I told them to sit on my porch, and I gave them some cokes, and I made them some popcorn while they waited for their mom.

They told me that they lost their keys for the third time and their mom was getting quite frustrated. And the next day, they came over and said that they were locked out of the house again. So, once again, I offered them cokes and gave them snacks.

It was funny because the little boy, who was about eight years old, took a dollar out of his pocket, and he put a dollar in my hand, and he said, "This is for you." I immediately said, "No, no, no," and I was giving it back to him, but I saw that he looked disappointed, and so I told the boy, "Okay, give me the dollar, and I receive it, and now I'm giving it back to you." The two boys looked at each other in utter shock!

I remember when I was a little girl, about nine years old, and I was walking home from school along with my younger brother and sister. We used to walk around the neighborhood on our way home. One day as we were walking, we saw this man on his porch sitting on his rocking chair.

He was an older man, maybe around sixty-five years. He said hi to us, and we said hi back. He offered us some candy, and, of course, we took it and said thank you. And after school we went past his house again, and lo and behold, he offered us more candy!

He lived about two blocks away from our house. Since I have a big family, we rarely got candy, so for us that was a huge treat! I can't tell you how good it felt when this man gave us candy! So, we would go back to his house quite often to see if he was there, and if he was, he would always give us something.

If he didn't have candy to give us, then he would give us something else, like a fruit or whatever he had. Ever feed an outside stray cat? I can say that we stray cats knew where to go! This man's name was Lefty. I will never forget Lefty. Unfortunately, I don't have a lot of great memories of what Christian people did for me or my family.

I don't believe that Lefty was a churchgoer either. But the other day I thought about him, and I realized that he is someone that I want to be like because he blessed my life in a positive way. So now I get to be a Lefty, and just as he has impacted life, I want to impact the lives of others.

We don't always have to invite someone to church to get them saved; after all, that was not how I got saved. I just knew that I was feeling empty, and I just wanted to be filled with something. I didn't know what; I just knew the way that I was feeling wasn't enough for me. I really didn't know a lot about religion or about God, for that matter, but I knew that I didn't like what I already had experienced in the church.

The Bible tells us that when we thirst and hunger after righteousness, we shall be filled (Matthew 5:6). I wanted answers as to why many churches are not fulfilling today. Anybody want to go to church? It's good to hear the Word of God at church, but right after church is over, all the people are rushing out the doors, and I can tell that they don't want to be bothered.

Sometimes when I talk to someone at church, I can see how they really struggle to pay attention to me. It's like they have this look like I'm wasting their time! Ya know what I mean? I remember when I used to answer the prayer lines for my church, I had so many lonely callers calling. Some of them would call just about every day. They just wanted to talk.

I would ask them if they had friends at church to talk to, and they would all tell me that no one in their church had time for them. Some of them would call several times a day just looking to talk...but rush, rush, rush, I had to get to the next caller!

There was this one particular girl who called a lot. She sounded so sweet, and I hated to hang up with her because I could tell that she, too, was quite lonely. We are so busy about our Father's business that we don't hear the still, small voice.

It's simply because we can't seem to find the time that we need to pray to the Father or spend time reading His Word; then we sit there and wonder why we are easily led astray when things get tough. We want so badly to prove to others that our way is right, yet we seem to be living on the far left!

We have no peace, no joy, and our smiles are so fake... after all, we don't want people to think that we are really miserable as we clap, shout, and dance in the church! Can you see how spiritual I really am? I remember when I fell in love with God for the first time! I so remember when...I couldn't stop talking about Him!

I remember when I used to brag about Him to anyone who would listen. People just knew that there was something different about me. It has become the norm for many Christians to be shouting in church and then cursing in public at the waitress who took too long to get them their check only because she was rushing to take other people's orders so she could feed her family!

We treat our bosses a lot better than our brothers and sisters in the Lord because, after all, our brothers and sisters really have nothing to offer us! We ignore our kids because we are too busy dancing, shouting, and looking important! Sometimes when I watch the news, I see tragedies that are happening, and then I see all the people rushing to get involved along with the first responders to help people who have been affected by these tragedies.

I don't believe that they are all Christians who are helping, but they just have a heart. But on the other hand, when somebody calls the church for help, well, they will hear, "Call my assistant and make an appointment!" My mom always depended on me when she was alive, and there were many times when I wouldn't get a break. At times I felt like I was being choked to death only because I didn't take time for myself.

I loved taking care of my mother because I love her with all my heart, but as stated before, I would end up forgetting about myself. I didn't really pay attention to myself. But then I realized that if I got too worn out, I would not be able to take care of my mom. God let me know that even that was wrong thinking. He showed me that I needed time to take care of myself just because I care about myself.

The Bible says that we are to love our neighbors as ourselves, and if we don't love ourselves, then we're probably not going to love our neighbors very much! Capiche. A person can't possibly give out what they don't have. When I started taking time out for myself, then I began to feel better about myself, and I also felt strong enough to take care of my mom. God let me know that He wants me to take care of myself because He loves me!

So many people give so much, and they may even love to do it, but since the Bible tells us that we are to love our neighbor as ourselves, then that means that we must make time to take care of ourselves. The bottom line is if we don't love ourselves and take care of ourselves, then why would our neighbor want to hang out with a rundown, useless person who doesn't care anything about themselves? And besides how good does that make God look anyway?

We are not to love ourselves in a vain way. Vanity means that we only love ourselves, and we expect everybody else to love us while we could care less about them! In order for us to love others, we have to love ourselves. That also means that we should have respect for ourselves. I had to go through that process of loving myself, and I must say that it was not easy for me to do only because I was so used to being a servant.

But I had to take care of myself in order for me to be a blessing to others and to my mom. After all, how can my light shine when I'm looking like a ragdoll? People who want to do so much for others end up forgetting about themselves, and then they end up, well...kind of like I was!

But as I prayed to God for guidance, then He was able to show me how He wanted me to live. He would show me what to read, and He even showed me how to get help for myself and also for my mom. I was in such bad shape that if I had ten things on my "to-do list," I only had the strength to accomplish one thing a day, even if it was something as simple as making a phone call.

That phone call would be the only thing that I had strength to do for the whole day. In other words, if I had to make one phone call or pay one bill, then I could only do one of them! And if I had to go to the store, to me, that was like climbing Mount Everett! For me to go somewhere, it would take me forever just to step out of the house!

I literally felt like I had a ton of weights on top of me! At times I actually felt like I was paralyzed! And when I did have to go somewhere, I literally would feel like I was lifting five hundred pounds of weight on my back, and the thing is that I only weigh a little bit. Many times, I would go without eating because it was easier for me not to eat than for me to take the time that I needed to cook for myself.

My mom ate different things than I did, and I would use all my strength and energy to cook for her, so by the time it came to me eating well, I was just too tired. I thank my Jesus that has all changed! Now when I have something that I have to do, even if I have ten things to do, I don't have a problem doing them. I may not get all ten things done, but I usually get the majority of it done.

I don't even have a long list of things to do anymore, and now I can do things as they come without feeling all weighed down. There were times when I didn't know where I was or who I was, for that matter! Then when I would look at my mom and see her in her condition, that just made me feel more lost!

How in the world was I supposed to get anything done feeling like that? I had laundry stacked up to the ceiling—clean and dirty! It took a week for me to decide if I was going to fold the clean towels or wash more dirty clothes! It took even longer for me to fold the sheets just because they were longer!

I would wear the same thing every day, and I barely had time to take showers; forget about combing my hair, and my hair is really long! The shoes that I wore were holey, and I don't mean holy either! I just didn't care about myself! But God let me know that things had to change, and He let me know that He didn't like what He saw when He saw me!

I really thought that me looking like I was, was pleasing to God, but He let me know differently! God created me, and when He did, it wasn't for me to be going the way that I was going. When King Solomon made the temple for God, they didn't leave it trashy, but they had certain people who made sure that it was very well taken care of. They had to clean it and make it shine ever so brightly!

According to the Bible, we are His temple, and He doesn't expect any less of our temple! So I knew that I needed to clean this temple up, but I didn't know how I was going to start. Too often people think that being selfless is weakness. People may feel that in order to be selfless, they have to give up everything about themselves. The Bible tells us that the husbands should love their wives as their own bodies. "So ought men to love their wives as their own bodies. He that loveth his wife loveth himself. For no man ever yet hated his own flesh; but nourisheth and cherisheth it, even as the Lord the church" (Ephesians 5:28–29).

God loves us so much that He sent His Son, Jesus, to die for us so that we could have life and have it more abundantly. I learned that every trial that God allows us to go through is so that we can have compassion for others who may be going through the same or similar thing. We go through trials so that we can share with others what we may have learned so that we can be an encouragement to them (2 Corinthians 1:4).

Did I want to go through what I have gone through? No way! I'd be crazy to say that I did! But I do want to help others, and if I can do that, then it makes what I have gone through so worth going through it! When I realized that I had to love my neighbor as myself, then I had to start doing things for myself and start taking care of myself.

I didn't go way out and do great stuff for myself or spend a lot of money on myself, but I did basic stuff that I needed to do to take care of myself. I started working out, taking vitamins, and cooking great meals for *meee*! I never wanted to go anywhere or do anything without my mom, but sometimes I needed to take some alone time for myself.

We really must know ourselves to be able to love who we are. I stated earlier that people try to be like someone else who they feel is perfect, but really God just wants us to be who He created us to be, and we must be able to love the person who God created so that we can love our neighbors as we love ourselves.

Chapter 19

The Lust of the Eyes

Love not the world, neither the things that are in the world. If any man love the world, the love of the Father is not in him. For all that is in the world, the lust of the flesh, and the lust of the eyes, and the pride of life, is not of the Father, but is of the world. And the world passeth away, and the lust thereof: but he that doeth the will of God abideth for ever.

1 John 2:15–17

Years ago, I went to visit my sister Abby, who lived in California. I have to say that when I got there, I was blown away! There were movie stars everywhere! There were great expensive restaurants with great food, and there were tons of gorgeous guys with money, and lots of it, I might add! I felt like I was a kid at Disneyland! So then I decided to pick up and move there! I must say that I was enjoying every bit of it—in the beginning, that is.

But as I hung around more, I realized that the rich men had enough money to buy...*me*...so they thought! After being there for a while, I began to see the phoniness in many rich people. I realized that even though people had money, some of them were quite miserable, and quite frankly, so was I! I had it all, and I was just as empty as they were...hmm. I dated, I partied, I drank, I danced, and I shopped till I dropped! I even traveled to the best places possible.

I had it all, yet I felt like I was falling into a deep, never-ending hole! I could never reach the point of satisfaction. I *cain't* get no satisfaction—I tried, I tried, I tried, and I tried...ha! The things that I felt would satisfy me, meaning the parties, the shopping, great food, and the men, made me realize that I was just lusting for the things that I didn't have because once I got those things, I still was not satisfied.

People only lust for things that they want but they cannot have. For instance, one time God told me to fast coffee. He didn't tell me to fast coffee for a day, a week, or even a month, but He had me fast coffee for a whole year! So, when I started that fast, I found myself having great cravings and a great desire for a cup of hot coffee, and let me tell you that I ever lusted it badly! Okay, for you, coffee lovers, go ahead and take a break and get yourself a cup right now! LOL! Better yet, why don't you try not to!

So after a year went by without having any coffee whatsoever, then when I was finally able to drink it, I realized that I didn't lust it anymore...the lust of the eyes! That's why so many times when a person meets another person who is really attractive, they begin to lust or desire that person, but once they get what they were lusting after, then things just don't seem to feel the same, and that desire that they once had for that person goes away. "I wonder why he doesn't look at me the way he used to." "I wonder why he looks at other women like he used to look at me."

A person can have four dogs, and when they see one that they don't have, it's amazing how they will adore that dog, and sometimes they adore it more than their own dog. Been there, done that! After I had gone on my coffee fast, I didn't go crazy for it, but instead, I appreciated my coffee, and now, I thank God every morning that I am able to drink it.

Sadly, sometimes, it takes losing something in order to fully appreciate it, whereas before we may have taken it for granted; whatever it may be, just try not having a refrigerator! People need to make themself visualize losing stuff in order to really appreciate them. Think of not having a computer; what would you ever do without it? The same goes with your cell phone, your job...and how about your mind? We simply take things for granted and don't realize just how many blessings we have until one day...your electricity goes out! No more water! Poof! It's gone!

Not too long ago, my electricity went out, and I tell you what, after it came back on, I was ever rejoicing and thanking God for His benefits! The more that I get to know God, the more I can appreciate what He does for little o' me! As I began to walk after the Spirit, then I began to see in the Spirit. And now I'm able to recognize those who are not walking after the Spirit but are walking after the flesh.

When you start operating in the Spirit, then you will begin to understand God more. God is a Spirit, and those who are in the flesh have those fleshly desires and the lust of the world. When a person walks after the flesh, they are not able to see the spiritual things because they are actually walking in darkness. The Bible says, "But the natural man receives not the things of the Spirit of God: for they are foolishness unto him: neither can he know them, because they are spiritually discerned" (1 Corinthians 2:14).

Once we decide to walk after the Spirit, then our minds will start understanding the deep things of God. I really don't miss having all those material things or costly things because God took out just about every desire that I had, and everything that I once loved, I don't love now. Everything that I used to desire I don't desire anymore only because they are not desirable to me anymore, period!

Think of your favorite restaurant that you love to eat at on special occasions, and think about what you really enjoy eating. If you get a chance to eat what you really enjoy every day, then after a while of having it so much, you will eventually get tired of eating what you once loved to eat. If you don't believe me, just find a rich person who has it all and ask them. In the book of Ecclesiastes, King Solomon will let you know that all is vanity!

When I go to the mall, I don't have a desire to even look at anything, much less buy anything. I stated earlier that I don't even care for jewelry anymore. When God says for us to take no thought, He really means it! I have peace because I don't desire things, or shall I say I don't lust after things. Don't believe me? Then just ask the lady who's always wearing different outfits at church. She's probably always thinking of what outfit she's going to buy to wear the next week; been there, done that! *All* is vanity!

I remember when I went to the doctor's office, and he told me that I couldn't eat wheat. Something crazy happened to me! After he told me that, all of a sudden, I started wanting foods that I didn't care for! I wanted pizza, hamburgers, and bread...bread...and more bread! I just wanted everything that had wheat in it; I just wanted it! I was craving it so badly, and what's funny was that some of these things that I craved, I never cared to eat them before I found out that I couldn't have them!

All of a sudden, I wanted to eat at Subway just because they served everything on bread! I had never cared to eat there before either, but I found out that I couldn't eat there, so then I really, really wanted it! I wanted to eat at Long John Silver's, and I never wanted to eat there before I found out that I couldn't. I found myself just wanting anything and everything with wheat!

And then after that, I found out that I couldn't have sugar. I never cared for candy, and all of a sudden, I found myself going through raging storming fits for candy! I never really ate ice cream, but all of a sudden, I just had to have it! I had cravings for the sweetest things in the world, and they were things that I didn't even care about before I found out that I couldn't have them. Can we talk?

I was so happy when I found sugar-free things and many gluten-free pastas and pizzas and even flour! But before I found those wonderfully made things, I just couldn't believe how I was going crazy desiring things that I had never ever desired before. I knew how I was feeling didn't even make sense to me, but my body was going out of control, and it just lusted for these things.

I never really ate cake, but after I found out that I couldn't have any, then when I would see one, it was like my body would go into total shock! I was withdrawing from things that I never had nor wanted! What's funny is one time I went to this place where they serve cinnamon rolls, big juicy hot cinnamon rolls with frosting melting and falling down to the earth! You know the place that I am talking about, don't you? Yes, Cinnabon!

When my mom and I went to the mall, we would stop by *Sin-a-bon* bakery every single time. But this time I knew that I was not supposed to eat them! So when we got there, I asked the owner of the store if they had insurance! He was from another country and didn't understand what I was asking, but I told him that I could not have sugar or wheat, and if something bad happened to me, I wanted to know if I would be insured! He laughed, but I wasn't laughing!

At the time, I didn't care what would have happened to me, and if I died, I was going to die happy! But God spared my life that day, and I really can say that after I ate a whole cinnamon bun, I was one happy camper! I felt a little bit weak after I ate it, but nevertheless, I lived to tell about it! Every week I would have to make a cake for my mom because she had to have a dessert every night.

I have to admit that one time I got really tempted; well, I was always tempted. I must say that my cakes turned out so good and ever so moist! And this time I gave in to that temptation, and I ate quite a few pieces until my body realized that it had better stop, and stop I did! I know this chapter is probably making you hungry, but try and go without everything that I have to go without and watch your body act and react in a bad way!

I'm not talking to the health freaks, but I may be talking to those who really should be health freaks! Sometimes God allows things to happen in order for us to take better care of ourselves. All things really do work together for the good! People simply want what they cannot have. Ever see a kid who wants everybody else's toy? Or how about someone who always wants someone else's food instead of what they ordered?

Ever go to an all-you-can-eat buffet restaurant? You just don't seem to want everything there—only because you can have everything there. Why do we pay $3 for a little snack in a vending machine when we could buy a big bag of that same snack for the same price at a grocery store? Shall I go on? God, help us!

Now I can say is all that I desire is to be with my Jesus! Nothing else matters to me. He really is all that I want! How can anyone even compare the things of this world to spending eternity with Jesus? What I thought I had wanted was what my flesh was craving, but when I allowed God to work in me, then He began removing everything out of me that needed to be removed, and after that, I began to have a clear vision of things.

What I thought would fill my emptiness—fame, title, expensive things, and even men—do not even come close to me having a relationship with the very One who created me! I now realize that God was the only One who could fill the emptiness and void in my life. When I began to see clearly, then I was able to understand that material things, or even what people may call "being in love" thing, were not able to fill the emptiness that I once had.

Many people find out that after they get what they thought would fill their void, the emptiness that they had is still there. And people who try to fill their void with a mate will probably feel emptier once they get their mate. Life will never be completely fulfilled without God. I realize now that my soul was craving for something more, and I didn't know that it was craving for God until God showed me.

It just feels so good not to desire the things of this world. Only God will make you complete in Him when you choose to give Him your full, undivided attention.

Chapter 20

The Effects of Words

"Death and life are in the power of the tongue: and they that love it shall eat the fruit thereof"

Proverbs 18:21

    Words are very powerful. I have learned that it is better not to say something if I am unsure what the outcome will be. When I got in heated conversation with someone, I would often call my oldest brother Ray, who recently went to be with the Lord; I would talk to him about my heated-up conversations, and every time he would always say, "Less is best."

    When I took care of my mom, there were so many things that I didn't understand. I didn't understand why she would start saying certain things that she never used to say before and why she did certain things that she never did before that were quite annoying. And since I was so accustomed to doing things in certain ways, I would sit there and argue with her.

    I found myself having too many heated arguments that would get me nowhere, but then it got me thinking about those words that my brother always told me, "Less is best." Our flesh always wants to have the last say in things only because it thinks that it is always right! Today we can look around and see how many intelligent people don't have all the right answers!

That really got me thinking about my very own answers. James 3 speaks about the tongue being such a little member, yet it can start great fires. "For in many things we offend all. If any man offend not in word, the same is a perfect man, and able also to bridle the whole body" (James 3:2). I like that scripture because it tells us how we can be a perfect man, and that right there gives me hope!

But the question remains, "How not to offend?" The answer is first to ask God for help. I'm finding out that practice does make perfect. The Bible says, "He that is slow to anger is better than the mighty; and he that ruleth his spirit than he that taketh a city" (Proverbs 16:32). As I have been applying these verses, I can say once again that the truth has definitely made me free!

Not only that, but it also has given me so much peace. Once again, God's Word really does work! I found myself not having to call anyone anymore about a heated-up argument in order to spew up my rightness! And that's because there really have not been too many heated-up arguments lately! Thank You, Jesus!

The truth is that I would only tell people about my heated-up conversations only to hear them tell me how right I was! I realized that even if I was on the right, and if I had the whole world agreeing with me, it wouldn't make a solitary difference if the person that I was arguing with and trying to convince that I was right would not agree with me and my rightness!

I know people who love to argue about how right they are, and I just happened to be one of them myself! But when I realized what I knew to be true could not penetrate the other person's mind, then I started keeping my rightness to myself. I did what was best for the both of us, which was to keep my mouth shut!

I wasted so much time thinking that I would actually convince a person that I was right by what I said to them until I realized that all my words fell to the ground. Some people will agree with you and tell you that you are right because that's just a nice way of telling a person to shut up! My mom used to tell me many times that I was right in that sense!

We must realize that words are very powerful! They can bring about healing to a person, or they can damage a person! Even when God used the prophet Elijah to do a great miracle with his sacrifice in front of four hundred and fifty of Jezebel's prophets of Baal, when he heard the words of Jezebel, saying that she was going to kill him, immediately he got scared, and he ran and hid.

Imagine someone telling you that you might have cancer. How would those words make you feel? There are so many children who have been crushed by their parents' words. Sometimes those words determine how they will end up. Not only words from a person can affect us, but we must remember that the devil never stops talking to us!

I just can't imagine living without God! It hurts my head when I see someone who is not saved and how they go through life hearing all kinds of negative words! They just don't know what to do with those words, but I thank God that I can go to Him! I've learned that me controlling my tongue has brought me a more peaceful life.

Every person has some form of rage in them. There's a beast in each and every one of us, and that beast is our flesh! When we get upset, that beast will show up and try to control the situation. The Bible tells us that "a soft word turneth away wrath: but grievous words stir up anger" (Proverbs 15:1). I have used that scripture in order to calm myself down, and let me tell you that it was not easy for me to do, but the scriptures work!

I was never a soft-spoken person, and for me to actually speak softly was like me holding my breath, kind of like the patient thing. When I first started speaking softly, I must admit that I was biting my tongue at the same time, and I bit it but good! I've learned that I can create my own atmosphere by how I speak.

There are people who will try to convince others that they have changed, but the way you really know that you've changed is when somebody else tells you. I remember how I used to get so upset over the littlest things and my words would get to flying everywhere! Now the little things that used to upset me don't even bother me. What's funny is that I actually find myself laughing over them. I am carefree!

There are people who call themselves Christians, who use sharp words when they rebuke people but have no love. They have the tongue of a serpent! They truly feel like they are doing God's work, but they are actually hurting the people that they are talking to. I used to be one of them!

The Bible says, "There is a way that seemeth right unto a man, but the end thereof are the ways of death" (Proverbs 16:25). It also says, "He that keepeth his mouth, keepeth his life: but he that openeth wide his lips shall have destruction" (Proverbs 13:3). People may think that by yelling at a person, the person will listen to them. Most of the time, when a person gets yelled at, telling them that they must do something, they will not do what the person wants them to do even if that person is right! And by yelling at them, they basically just made an enemy.

Parents who scream at their kids don't realize that their words go in one ear and out the other... "Didn't I tell you?" "How many times do I have to tell you?" "And, ye fathers, provoke not your children to wrath: but bring them up in the nurture and admonition of the Lord" (Ephesians 6:4).

People want to hear what they want to hear, and that's really sad! "Just tell me that I'm right!" If every child only pays attention to what they want to hear, they will end up in bad shape! "Don't touch that knife." "Don't put your hand in the electric socket." "Look both ways before you cross the street." "Finish your homework." "Do not text and drive."

I am amazed when I hear someone say such nasty things to me in order to get a reaction from me; now I can tune them out in a heartbeat minute! I must admit that I had quite a mouth on me! For me not to speak back is a miracle in itself! I'm not saying that I don't ever speak up, but I'm saying that now I don't blow up when I speak up. I admit that there have been times when I may blow up, but nowhere near like I used to.

Now when someone uses sharp words when they speak to me in order to get me riled up, I hold up my shield of faith, and I stay calm. Their words are like annoying flies that are flying around my head, but I know how to use the fly swatter! That's exactly what I do with those sharp words! Bye-bye, Beelzebub!

So many relationships have been broken because of the words that have been spoken to one another. There was a time when I used to always ponder on the ugly words that people would say to me. Their words would cut like a knife! I would meditate on them day and night, so much so that I could not rest. I just wanted these people to be punished severely for what they had said.

Have you ever said something in a heated-up argument to someone that you really care for and ended up regretting saying those words that you really didn't mean, and it just hurt them so badly that they couldn't get over it? Well, I could probably safely say that everyone has, unless they are mute or maybe saints. Dunno. Those are fiery darts, by the way, and they sting!

We must remember that we are still living in this flesh suit that fleshes out from time to time. Many times, people really don't mean to say what they say, but they simply cannot help it. When people say something to a person that makes them feel uncomfortable, the other person automatically wants to lash out in order for them to feel less uncomfortable.

"You said I'm slow; well, you are unreliable!" "You said that my food wasn't that good; well, your breath stinks!" Then they will sit there and ponder on the hurtful words that were spoken to them. They just can't understand why the person that they care about said what they said. They will stay hurt, and the hurt will turn to anger, and they can't seem to forget or forgive that person.

Sometimes it's hard for a person to take criticism of any sort, and because of that, the other person won't say anything, and they will keep eating their tasteless food. Then after a while, they stop talking altogether. I would always ask my mom how her food tasted, and if she didn't like it, I wanted her to let me know right away because I wanted her to enjoy her food! I aimed to please! After all that's how I learned to cook so well; after all who wants to serve other people food that their spouse doesn't like?

I wish I could say that once a person gets saved, they will never hurt another person with their words, but that is not the case at all. C'mon, even Jesus fleshed out many times! Not only did He turn over tables, but He went to rebuking but good! "You serpents, you generation of vipers!" God fleshed out many times in the beginning. "Moses, I'm gonna kill them all and start all over!" "And the Lord said unto Moses, I have seen this people, and, behold, it is a stiffnecked people: Now therefore let me alone, that my wrath may wax hot against them, and that I may consume them: and I will make of thee a great nation" (Exodus 32:9–10).

The apostle Paul said, "I die daily" (1 Corinthians 15:31). There was a good reason for that! Paul and Barnabas got into a great dispute over John Mark to the point that they had to separate from each other. "And the contention was so sharp between them, that they departed asunder one from the other: and so Barnabas took Mark, and sailed unto Cyprus" (Acts 15:39).

Many times, people will say hurtful things because they are upset about something else. They don't mean to lash out at you or hurt you, and until you realize that, then you will continue to live in a hurtful and angry state of mind. Peter asked Jesus, "How many times must I forgive? Up to seven times?" And Jesus said seventy times seven (Matthew 18:21).

Basically, what Jesus was saying is that people will always make mistakes. I want to be clear and let you know that I am in no way pertaining to abusive people! Some people are just hateful and vindictive and just want to hurt other people and make them feel like trash so they can look and feel good about themselves! They could care less if they hurt you!

I'm talking about those who really care about you and regretfully say the wrong things and who are truly sorry for saying hurtful words. We are growing every day, and we should be dying to our flesh every day; we should also be changing through the process as well. We must also realize that these are the last days that we are living in.

A lot of bad things are happening, and a lot of people are going through really tough times. Many people are struggling to just make ends meet. Many people are struggling with their health. Many people are struggling with their jobs. We are living in hard times, and it's getting really hard for people. That's the reason you hear about so many drive-by shootings! You must really be careful not to offend anyone on the road!

When your loved ones are going through tough times, they actually feel like they are on fire, and you will feel the heat, which can bring about a heated argument. Christians who are being refined by fire are burning up. I know the feeling indeed! It doesn't feel an ounce bit good!

So please don't let bitter words be the last words spoken or the last words remembered. It's always good after a heated argument for people to take time away from each other to cool down and then make up. Remember less really is best! After all it's much better to make up than to break up!

Chapter 21

Pruning Is a Must!

"I am the true vine, and my Father is the husbandman. Every branch in me that beareth not fruit he taketh away: and every branch that beareth fruit, he purgeth it, that it may bring forth more fruit"

John 15:1–2

John chapter 15 talks about bearing fruit. Since I have been reading the Bible, I'm finding out what needs to be removed from my life. Since God has been working in me, I have to say that I feel like I have been going through the process of being pruned! I feel like I have been cut, chopped, snipped, and clipped! I thank God that I can also see the results of the pruning! God must prune everything out of our lives that is not of Him in order for us to bear good fruit.

> *Now the works of the flesh are manifest, which are these; Adultery, fornication, uncleanness, lasciviousness, Idolatry, witchcraft, hatred, variance, emulations, wrath, strife, seditions, heresies, Envyings, murders, drunkenness, revellings, and such like: of the which I tell you before, as I have also told you in*

time past, that they which do such things shall not inherit the kingdom of God.

Galatians 5:19–21

"But the fruit of the Spirit is love, joy, peace, longsuffering, gentleness, goodness, faith, Meekness, temperance: against such there is no law. And they that are Christ's have crucified the flesh with the affections and lusts. If we live in the Spirit, let us also walk in the Spirit" (Galatians 5:22–25).

Psalm 51:5 says that we were born or conceived in sin. Before we got born again, we lived after the flesh, but when we got born again, then we had to learn how to live after the Spirit. To live after the Spirit is contrary to how we were born. In some islands people drive on the opposite side of the street. I went to a few islands that did that, and I must say that I didn't feel comfortable at all! I was really scared, especially when we were driving on the curves in the mountains! Now try doing that with your whole life!

What seems to be a way of normal living is not normal according to God's Word. We work so very hard to get where we are and to get the things that we have, but when we read the Bible, it tells us that "it is more blessed to give than to receive" (Acts 20:35). Remember a child's first word is not always ma...but mine!

Many people in relationships feel that if a person truly loves them, they will give them what they want; that's exactly how I used to feel! If that's true, then tell me, who's the giver and who's the taker? When we were born, we were born with a mind of nothing, and our minds go any which way!

We see something that we want, and then we figure out a way to get it! Man wants woman until...woman wants kids until...they actually get one! But when we truly want God, we really must be willing to give God everything: our desires, our future, our will, and even our thoughts—thank God for that one! And we also must obey a God that we don't see. How can this be?

We can read the Bible and see just how much the people in the Bible's flesh got them. It's so mind-boggling to read the Old Testament about God's people rejecting Him over and over and over again! And the real mind-boggling part is that when the people repented, God would bless them tremendously! But when they rebelled, then they would suffer tremendously, and yet, they kept choosing to suffer...tremendously! These books are an example to show us where sin will get us.

> *For if God spared not the angels that sinned, but cast them down to hell, and delivered them into chains of darkness, to be reserved unto judgment; And spared not the old world, but saved Noah the eighth person, a preacher of righteousness, bringing in the flood upon the world of the ungodly; And turning the cities of Sodom and Gomorrah into ashes condemned them with an overthrow, making them an ensample unto those that after should live ungodly.*
>
> 2 Peter 2:4–6

We see the good, the bad, and the ugly! Whose life will we follow, and which way will we choose to live? What's even crazier for me is when I read how God's people lived so wickedly and then read how so many times God is pleading with His people to do right. Seriously? God is also telling them that if they live right, then He will forgive their sins and greatly bless them, but sadly, so many times, they ignore God and end up being severely punished by Him!

When God's people chose to walk right, God would miraculously show up, whether it was during the sacrifices or during wars. God would fight their battles, and they would win big time! I have been battling on how to become more like Jesus and how to put on His mind so that my mind would just not exist, but no matter what I do, this obnoxious mind of mine seems to always show up!

"Oh no, my dog is sick!" God why? Something so small tries to take a toll on my little teeny-weeny hollow mind! "What am I going to do! My dog's going to die!" It always seems to be the little things that get my little mind going! Fear is so opposite of God's mind! When we fear, we may not realize it, but we are so opposite of God. We can easily believe the lies of the devil more than we believe God's report. Why?

An irritated spirit is another thing that keeps us from walking in the fruit of the joy of the Lord and in peace. When two people get together and live under the same roof, whether it be a spouse, a mother, a sister, a brother, or even a roommate, then they can expect to be annoyed by each other in one way or another. People talk too much, people talk too loud, people don't like the same things, and for sure people do not think alike!

I don't know if opposites really attract. My relationships never lasted, whether they were opposite of me or the same as me. Personally, I would rather someone agree with me and like what I like than have someone try to tell me that spinach tastes really, really good when I absolutely hate it! Just leave me alone already! I like corn!

I realize that people are not going to be like me. My mom rarely liked what I ate, and that's why I had to cook separate meals. And then later on in her life she got even more finicky about what she ate. She hated gluten-free stuff; I have no choice but to eat that stuff! Do I wish my mom would have eaten what I ate…you bet I do!

When I began to see myself getting irritated and frustrated about my mom wanting whatever she wanted only because I had to go out of my way to get her what she wanted, then I realized that I needed to be worked on big time! I realized that my irritated, frustrated attitude was keeping me from receiving what God had for me.

I read this verse, "Let the words of my mouth, and the meditation of my heart, be acceptable in thy sight, O Lord, my strength, and my redeemer" (Psalm 19:14). Once again "how to?" Purge, baby, purge! We must be purged in order for us to change and for us to go from darkness into God's marvelous light. Nobody wakes up changed!

Again, I believed that I was a really good Christian until God's Word shined brightly in my face! It was the weirdest thing when I saw myself because I was totally different than who I thought I was. I felt that because I attended church faithfully and volunteered a lot and became a leader and prayed for people and danced and shouted, I was ready for heaven. I truly believed that!

When I think about this now, it is so scary for me when I realize that I was not ready to go to heaven, and it scared me to death! How could I not have known the truth when I was so involved with the church? How could I not have seen the light all those years? Everything was going great for me, and even the blessings were none other than great! But trials began, and that was when I was able to see...*me*!

Even now when I think about where I am, my stomach gets sick! I thank God that I'm not where I used to be, but I still know that I'm not where I want to be. One time my sister Abby told me that I don't have a selfish bone in my body. That's because I am always thinking about her and what she needs, whereas before, I could care less!

The thing is that she doesn't know that sometimes I don't want to do things for her, but I do them because I want to bear fruit. And because the fact that I'd rather not do things for her at times makes me feel very yucky! I'm continually fighting thoughts of selfishness and fighting the feelings of not wanting to do things for other people.

For instance, my mom used to always ask me to heat up her coffee every thirty minutes. She would take thirty minutes before she took one drink, and when she wanted me to heat her coffee up for the fiftieth time, I can honestly say that I was not a happy camper! I would tell her that she needed to drink her coffee when it was hot! I had to fight those not-wanting-to-heat-her-coffee-fifty-times-a-day feelings!

As God continued to purge me, I started heating her coffee with a smile, and after a while it just became automatic for me to do. Then, after a while, I found myself asking her if she wanted me to heat her coffee versus her having to ask me. I noticed that I began doing things for my mom out of love and compassion, and I started being very gentle with her.

God was purging me from the ugly, heartless, selfish, and irritated person that I was. When God purges me, I feel like I am being skinned alive, but from the inside, and it doesn't feel good! The Bible often talks about the circumcision of the heart, and that's kind of how it feels! Not only that, but it seems like I am being tested and tried just about every day; sometimes I pass, and sometimes I don't.

This dumb mind of mine also tends to worry far too much! God will prove Himself to me time and time again, and yet this pathetic mind gets to worrying! When will it stop already? I really wish I could reprogram this thing! But I can say that when I pray, I notice the worries fade away, and when I wake up, the worries just show up unannounced! "Hi there!" and I will say,

"Shut up, you lowdown rotten dog!" Once again, I get to casting down those imaginations.

I can honestly say that through this purging process, I can see my fruit coming forth. I can feel the change, and I can see the results. As a bush of roses grows and is required to be cut, so it goes with us! We must be able to bear the purging and the pruning in order for the fruit to come. This is not an option if we truly want to be God's disciples. "Herein is my Father glorified, that ye bear much fruit; so shall ye be my disciples" (John 15:8).

The apostle Paul says that when he does good, evil is present. People told me that they could see a change in me; I let them know that even though I look like I am doing better, I am still biting my tongue! I tell them that doing the right thing will not always be easy, but I choose to do the right thing.

For me to bear fruit has been like me climbing a mountain. I want to reach the top of that mountain, but it is very hard. I can't ride a helicopter and take the easy way up, and unfortunately that's not the way it works. We must continue to press on as we "press toward the mark for the prize of the high calling of God in Christ Jesus" (Philippians 3:14).

There will always be a voice in our ear telling us to do the right thing, and there will always be a voice in our other ear telling us to do the wrong thing. One voice is directing us to the light, and the other one is directing us into total darkness. I notice that the more that I choose to do the right thing, then after a while, it becomes natural for me to do, and that's when the fruit showed up!

"But he that received seed into the good ground is he that heareth the word, and understandeth it; which also beareth fruit, and bringeth forth, some an hundredfold, some sixty, some thirty" (Matthew 13:23). I won't be satisfied until I reach the hundredfold!

Chapter 22

Daddy Chastises

> *"All scripture is given by inspiration of God, and is profitable for doctrine, for reproof, for correction, for instruction in righteousness: That the man of God may be perfect, thoroughly furnished unto all good works"*
>
> 2 Timothy 3:16–17

When I first read about how God punished the people in the Old Testament, at first, I felt like they totally deserved the punishment that they got. God had given the people so many warnings, even through the prophets, and yet it seemed like they just didn't care. They killed many of the prophets because they didn't want to hear what God was saying.

But as I read the Bible over and over again, it hit me, and I realized that in our flesh we really cannot do anything on our own. They could stop sinning for a while because they feared God and His wrath. I don't believe they obeyed so much out of love for God but out of fear. I don't know if I could even love God without His Holy Spirit dwelling in me.

The Bible says that "the love of God is shed abroad in our hearts by the Holy Ghost" (Romans 5:5). So it takes the Holy Ghost to fill us with God's love. Have you ever tried to love someone on your own by forcing yourself?

The Bible says, "No man can even say that Jesus is Lord but by the Holy Ghost" (1 Corinthians 12:3).

It takes the Holy Spirit to transform us into a new person. People can easily condemn or judge the people who sin against God, but as I continue to study God's Word, I realize that the people in the Old Testament and even in the New Testament did not have God's Spirit dwelling inside of them until Jesus died on the cross and gave us His Holy Spirit.

I stated earlier when Adam and Eve ate the forbidden fruit, then sin arose in them, and it made us all the sinful way that we are. I can say that even today there are times that I find myself getting in the flesh, and I tend to think bad thoughts. Some may be about other people who did me wrong, or I may start to fear or worry, or I just may get stupid thoughts of thinking that I am way better than someone else!

Before Jesus departed, He told His disciples to wait because they still did not have the Holy Spirit dwelling inside of them. That's why Peter denied Jesus three times, and the other disciples doubted, feared, and ran away when Jesus was taken. Even though they walked with Jesus for three years and saw all the great miracles that He did, they still feared.

But when Jesus left, then they were able to receive His Holy Spirit in them that raised Christ from the dead. "But if the Spirit of him that raised up Jesus from the dead dwell in you, he that raised up Christ from the dead shall also quicken your mortal bodies by his Spirit that dwelleth in you" (Romans 8:11).

The Bible says, "There is therefore now no condemnation to them which are in Christ Jesus, who walk not after the flesh, but after the Spirit" (Romans 8:1). I talked about the fruit of the Spirit earlier. We can see that fruit of the Spirit is contrary to walking after the flesh. "Because the carnal mind is enmity against God: for it is not subject to the law of God, neither indeed can be. So then they that are in the flesh cannot please God" (Romans 8:7–8).

In the Old Testament, we read how God tried everything to get His people to walk upright. When they repented and followed God's law, then God would bless them; sadly, that didn't last too long, and the people would go back into sin. I don't know what I would do without God's Holy Spirit! Not having God's Spirit would be like me going without breathing.

I can't even imagine not having His Holy Spirit dwelling in me, nor can I imagine trying to walk a godly life in my flesh. The Bible not only tells us that God punished the people, but it tells us how He punished them. As I stated earlier, He punished the people in the Old Testament to set an example for us.

> *But with many of them God was not well pleased: for they were overthrown in the wilderness. Now these things were our examples, to the intent we should not lust after evil things, as they also lusted. Neither be ye idolaters, as were some of them; as it is written, The people sat down to eat and drink, and rose up to play. Neither let us commit fornication, as some of them committed, and fell in one day three and twenty thousand.*
>
> *Neither let us tempt Christ, as some of them also tempted, and were destroyed of serpents. Neither murmur ye, as some of them also murmured, and were destroyed of the destroyer. Now all these things happened unto them for examples: and they are written for our admonition, upon whom the ends of the world are come.*
>
> 1 Corinthians 10:5–11

"Jesus Christ is the same today yesterday and forever" (Hebrews 13:8). That simply means that He does not change. I've heard preachers preach that God will not punish us, but the Bible tells us that He chastises those who He loves. "For whom the Lord loveth he chasteneth, and scourgeth every son whom he receiveth" (Hebrews 12:6).

"Wherefore, my beloved, as ye have always obeyed, not as in my presence only, but now much more in my absence, work out your own salvation with fear and trembling" (Philippians 2:12). "Serve the Lord with fear, and rejoice with trembling" (Psalms 2:11). We must not forget that God is a judge, and soon we will all be judged by Him.

I've heard preachers say that God did not create evil, but I knew that wasn't true because I had already read that He did. "The Lord hath made all things for himself: yea, even the wicked for the day of evil" (Proverbs 16:4).

In Genesis 2:9 God placed the tree of knowledge and good and evil in the garden, and by the way, He created hell. Hell doesn't sound like a good place to go, but nevertheless, God created that place.

People want to assume who God is, and they want to make Him to be who He is not. If you truly want to know God, you can. It is written! For anyone to deny any of God's Word is to deny God, period! The Bible says that God came in the flesh. "And without controversy great is the mystery of godliness: God was manifest in the flesh, justified in the Spirit, seen of angels, preached unto the Gentiles, believed on in the world, received up into glory" (1 Timothy 3:16). He came to destroy the works of the devil (1 John 3:8). "Behold, I give unto you power to tread on serpents and scorpions, and over all the power of the enemy: and nothing shall by any means hurt you" (Luke 10:19).

He gave us His Holy Spirit to guide us into truth. "Howbeit when he, the Spirit of truth, is come, he will guide you into all truth: for he shall not speak of himself; but whatsoever he shall hear, that shall he speak: and he will shew you things to come" (John 16:13). He also gave us the grace or the power to serve and obey Him. And on top of that, He even gave us the power to do the things that Jesus did.

And when we choose to go against God, then we can expect to be whipped by God.

> *Of how much sorer punishment, suppose ye, shall he be thought worthy, who hath trodden under foot the Son of God, and hath counted the blood of the covenant, wherewith he was sanctified, an unholy thing, and hath done despite unto the Spirit of grace?*
>
> *For we know him that hath said, Vengeance belongeth unto me, I will recompense, saith the Lord. And again, The Lord shall judge his people. It is a fearful thing to fall into the hands of the living God.*
>
> Hebrews 10:29–31

And God will show mercy to those who fear Him. Like a father pitieth his children, so the Lord pitieth at them that fear him. But the mercy of the Lord is from everlasting to everlasting upon them that fear him, and his righteousness unto children's children; To such as keep his covenant, and to those that remember his commandments to do them.

Psalm 103:13, 17–18

When I hear people say things like they are mad at God, I know that they really don't know God at all. I remember how I used to always yell at God before I got saved, but as I read the Bible, I can see that I was just crazy talking to God like that! I thank God that He's merciful even to the ignorant! I will never understand why God puts up with us, but I am so glad that He does!

In 1 Corinthians 5, Paul talks about a man who committed fornication with his father's wife and says that that man should be delivered unto Satan for the destruction of the flesh so that his spirit may be saved. He didn't say that he delivered the man to Satan to kill him. He was turning him over to Satan so that Satan would mess up his body or bring about an affliction on his body so that he would repent.

King David said, "It is good for me [to be] afflicted that I might learn thy statutes" (Psalm 119:71). Once again God does not want anyone to perish, but He just wants everyone to repent. The reason God punishes people is to get their attention so they can repent from their evil ways and turn back to God so that God can bless them and save them from eternal hell.

When people do wrong, then they are hurting other people. God's commandments are placed there for us to follow so that we would stop hurting other people, just like the law of the land is used for people to stop hurting other people. If someone comes inside another person's home to rob them or to bring harm to them, then they deserve to be punished by law. Parents punish their children for doing wrong, and the same goes with God.

God is a just God, and He's not going to look the other way and ignore our wrongdoings. When people break the law of the land, they get ticketed, they get their privileges suspended, they get fined, they go to jail, or they may even end up in prison. Those are all God's principles as well.

Sadly, we can see today that those who are doing evil are the ones getting rewarded, and those who do good are being punished. That's because we are living in the last days, and the Bible tells us it would be like this. Today we hear many so-called Christian people say that people who talk about living according to God's Word are religious fogies and are very judgmental, and the world says that we are haters.

When I read the Psalms, I could not believe how King David was chastised. When King David committed the horrible sin of killing a soldier so that he could marry the soldier's wife, he got a punishment for life through his children. You won't hear that preached much, but sadly what you will hear is that God doesn't mind when people sin and compare sin to King David's sin, and they will leave out the judgment that King David got from that sin.

After King David sinned, the prophet Nathan pronounced the judgment that the sword would never depart from King David's house and said that God would rise up evil against His house (2 Samuel 12:9–12).

One of His sons raped his daughter; one of his sons murdered his other son and even tried to kill King David, and that son was killed. Have I been whipped by God? O yes, I have! Was it a slap on the hand...? *Not*! God is merciful, but He will not be mocked! We must realize that when Daddy chastises, it's only to bring about good for us even though it may not feel like it, but you can be sure that in the end, it will work together for our good!

Chapter 23

For All Have Sinned and Come Short

As I have been going through a pruning process and bearing fruit, I know that I am being changed from glory to glory; however, I have not been perfected. I feel like my insides are ready to explode, and that, my friend, does not feel very good! I would love to go home to my Jesus, but as of now, I don't believe that I am quite ready. The other day I lied. I have been doing really good in not lying, but now that I lied, I feel horrible and horribly sick about it!

A few years ago, my sister Abby came to live with me. She told me that when she was living in California, she hurt her ankle. She went to the doctors, and they could not figure out what was wrong with her, and so they prescribed her pain medication. Since they could not find out what was wrong with her ankle and her ankle kept bothering her, they kept refilling her medication until she became addicted.

Many of us know of someone who has struggled in that area, and unfortunately some have had loved ones who didn't make it. My sister lived a hard life because of that. When I watched her struggle with her addiction, I always wondered if she would ever be whole. She always loved God, and she would always pray to God for her deliverance.

So, when I looked at her, I just couldn't imagine what she was going through. She had spent all her money on drugs, so I took her in my house. When she moved in with me, she would help me with our mother, but she couldn't seem to shake the addiction. Years before that, she told me that she and her daughter and our niece were taking a trip, and while she was in the car, she had overdosed, and she was unconscious.

So they took her to a hospital, where she died. My sister told me that they had to resuscitate her three times, and after that, she came to; then she went in a coma for three days. The doctors told her daughter that she had lost twelve hours of oxygen and that she would be a vegetable if she woke up. I remember praying for her along with my dad and mom and she did wake up. Not only that, but she woke up in her right mind. But sadly, that did not stop her from doing drugs!

So, when I watched her, sometimes I wondered if she would ever be completely delivered. I guess I could say that I was a doubting Thomas! I have by no means pushed her into seeking God or into praying, but she has been doing that on her own. I didn't make her get up in the morning to go to church, but to my surprise, she would get up on her own, and she was not a happy camper when we missed church!

I don't want to push anyone into going to church or serving God because that's what my father tried to do with me. I learned through my own experience that it doesn't work that way. I'm talking about adults, not children. My father and mother instilled God in me when I was young, and even though we attended a church that was full of religious haters, I still felt the presence of God there.

I would get so blessed during the praise and worship service because the anointing was in no doubt there, and that has never left me. I also went to Sunday school and learned about the Bible. The Bible says, "Train up a child in the way he should go: when he is old, he will not depart from it" (Proverbs 22:6). When I got older, I ran away from church and from God as fast as I could!

I ran away because of all those man-made rules that my dad had learned from church and pushed them on me. But I can say that because I had experienced God's awesome presence at the church, it was like God never left me even when I was living for the devil. What's crazy is that when I was in the world, I would have dreams and visions from God!

These dreams and visions were so real to the point that I would experience His awesome presence in my dreams, and there were times that I woke up speaking in tongues and even prophesying. I remember one time, after having a vision, I had to go to work the next morning, and I couldn't stop speaking in tongues all the way to work!

I had gone to the nightclub the night before I had that vision, mind you, but that didn't stop me from going to nightclubs. I went back to the club a few days later because that was where I had fun! It wasn't until many years later that I received Christ as my Lord and Savior. I am saying this to let you know that God is the One who saves and God alone!

Nobody can save anyone! People really need to quit trying to save other people! The best remedy for someone to get saved is for us to tell them about Jesus and be a witness and an example to them. We must pray that God touches their heart to receive what we have told them and for them to accept Jesus as their Lord and Savior.

God is the only One who can set people free! We must remember that their heart is in the hand of the Lord, and God is the One who directs the heart of people. I used to think that people in a relationship who lived together should get married right away so they could be saved. I realized that even though people who are living together should get married, there are a lot of other things that they may be doing that may be keeping them from going to heaven, such as lying, cheating, stealing, and so forth.

I have been feeling so down from lying the other day, and I'm so upset at myself! I lied because of fear that if I told the truth, I would not have favor. That just made me realize that I'm still half-baked! I can say that I haven't lied in a very long time, but for some reason this lie came out! I thank God that He began the work in me and He will finish it!

God has delivered me from so many things, and I can honestly say that I feel His presence so greatly! I can actually feel Him inside of me, and I can also say that sometimes He burns me up to the point that I can't stand up! "For our God is a consuming fire" (Hebrews 12:29). He really is!

I used to hate looking at people who call themselves Christians and live like the devil. The reason that I got so very frustrated was that it made me feel that people cannot change no matter what... there goes me doubting again! I keep forgetting that we were born in sin, and therefore, we live like the devil until we get born again.

I desperately want to be like my Jesus! I want to be His perfect little girl, but I know that I cannot be His perfect little girl on my own and without Him. I cannot do anything on my own, no matter how badly I want to. Now when I may sin in certain areas, instead of getting down on myself, I just need to realize that I'm a work in progress.

"But now, O Lord, thou art our father; we are the clay, and thou our potter; and we all are the work of thy hand" (Isaiah 64:8). The key is for me to believe that what God starts, He will complete! I must be confident! We must acknowledge where we need God's help and continue to pray for His help in whatever area of our lives that we may be struggling in.

As I watched my sister struggling, it made me weep as I saw her desperately trying to do good. I just continued to pray to God to continue to work in her. When she was living with my mom and me, she got to the point that I felt that my mom and my life were in danger. I had to kick her out of my house, but I never stopped praying for her.

A few years later, I heard that she quit taking drugs, and I brought her back to live with me. I must say that it wasn't easy because even though she was not back on her drugs, she still was the same person. She had her ways, and nothing that I said mattered to her! She was seeking God, and God was working in her, and all I could do was pray for her and pray for me also!

Once again, we were both taking care of my mom, but because she still had her ways, we had many heated-up arguments. I didn't know what I was going to do, but I knew that prayer worked! Later on, I realized that God was using her to work on me!

What amazed me was when I prayed to God for her to change in certain areas, then she would tell me that God revealed to her that she needed to change in the area that I was praying for! This happened a lot! She used to constantly argue with me about anything and everything, and I went to God and prayed about that.

Not long after that, she told me that she dreamt that she was arguing with me in her dream. She said that she heard a thunderous noise, and it really scared her! She told me that God wanted her to stop arguing with me. God has done a miraculous work in both of our lives, and now we are both on fire for God, living together in peace and harmony. Prayer works! God's Word works!

What's great is that I can see God's handiwork right before my eyes! When I see how corrupt the world is today and see how many of the churches have been deceived, it makes me wonder how many people are truly saved. I stated how so many people have such high expectations of men and women who are in high places who have been led astray and have fallen.

But as I look at myself and I see my shortcomings, I know that I would not want anyone to look up to me and think that I was somebody great, never! Even John the Baptist refused to be lifted up, but instead he said that he had to decrease! Just as children are not born mature, neither are Christians born mature when they get born again.

Jesus chose twelve grown men to be His disciples, and even though He trained them for three years, they still had to wait to be filled with the Holy Ghost before they could do anything. Jesus didn't start preaching till He was thirty years old. As stated earlier, Jesus had to learn obedience, and we certainly are not exempt! I can safely say that from reading the Bible, there is quite a lot to learn!

We all want to reach a higher height, but just as with anything that a person may want to succeed in, it will take plenty of time, patience, and practice; it will even take plenty of failings! Many people who had great accomplishments failed miserably before they succeeded, but the key is not to give up!

I know people who have taken a test for their driver's license who have failed, but that never stopped them from retaking the test. That's because they knew that, eventually, they would have a driver's license in their hands. They just had to study harder and concentrate a little bit more and definitely learn from the mistakes that they made.

When a person gets saved, they must realize that before they got saved, they were living a certain way for many years. I stated earlier that I used to lie a whole lot and I did that for many years of my life. Though I am getting better at not lying, I will not give up praying for the day that I will not lie another lie!

Although God has delivered me from so much as only He could have, I still have to do my part because faith without works is dead. "Even so faith, if it hath not works, is dead, being alone" (James 2:17). God told Noah to build an ark, and He flooded the earth because the people were so wicked. So He started up with Noah and his sons and told them to be fruitful, multiply, and replenish the earth.

Unfortunately, things got bad once again, and sin became the norm, and once again they forgot about God. When you don't teach your children about God, then they won't teach theirs, and so forth and so on, and so goes today. Years later, God appeared to Abram and told him to leave his home.

When God called Abram, he and his family were serving other gods and believed in them. They had different gods for different things. They had fertility gods and prosperity gods. They had sun gods and moon gods, and they worshipped these gods. Many of these gods were figures that they made with their hands.

When God told Abram to leave his home, He didn't tell him where to go, but He told him that He would bless him greatly. So, Abram took a step of faith, and he obeyed God. If Abram had never left, then he would not have received the many blessings that he received because of his faith in God and for his obedience to God.

> *And the Lord appeared unto him, and said, Go not down into Egypt; dwell in the land which I shall tell thee of: Sojourn in this land, and I will be with thee, and will bless thee; for unto thee, and unto thy seed, I will give all these countries, and I will perform the oath which I sware unto Abraham thy father;*
>
> *And I will make thy seed to multiply as the stars of heaven, and will give unto thy seed all these countries; and in thy seed shall all the nations of the earth be blessed; Because that Abraham obeyed my voice, and kept my charge, my commandments, my statutes, and my laws.*
>
> Genesis 26:2–5

People may say that because Abraham just believed, that is the reason he became great. But here we read the reason he became great was because he obeyed God. So, when we believe that God is doing a work in us, then we must do our part. We must submit to God, resist the devil, and believe that he will flee from us. We must do our part, pray, and believe that God will answer our prayers as His Word says He will.

We must read the Bible and believe that when we have God's Word in us, then we have God's power operating in us. We must believe the scripture, "I can do all things through Christ which strengtheneth me" (Philippians 4:13). As I stated before, when a person first gives their life to God, they won't change overnight, but it will be a process. So, when they are growing, there will be times when they will fail God.

When I first gave my life to God and I sinned, I felt horrible! I didn't want to even look at God because I had felt so shameful! I want to let you know that it's good for us to feel bad when we sin against God. When we hurt someone that we love so much, it hurts us, and if we love God so much, it should hurt us also.

"For thou desirest not sacrifice; else would I give it: thou delightest not in burnt offering. The sacrifices of God are a broken spirit: a broken and a contrite heart, O God, thou wilt not despise" (Psalm 51:16–17). The great thing is that God's Holy Spirit will convict us of our wrongdoing before we may sin and even after we may sin, and when we come to God with a sincere and repented heart, then God will forgive us.

When you sin and you keep asking God to forgive you in all sincerity, then you will notice that the things that once had you bound will start decreasing, just like the lying spirit, which has decreased tremendously, and that goes with any sin. Just remember when we confess our sins, God is faithful, and He will forgive us and continue to cleanse us.

We must believe this scripture, but first, there must be a confession. God is a merciful God, and I would not dare take God's forgiveness for granted. "Be not deceived; God is not mocked: for whatsoever a man soweth, that shall he also reap" (Galatians 6:7).

Not too long ago, my sister sent me a couple of videos from YouTube about men who died and went to hell. Look up "Shot twice then into hell." "I was a Chicago gang member and went to hell after being shot twice" (Dominic's testimony). The other one is called "7 TIERS OF TORMENT IN HELL" (R. Cook's testimony).

I listened to them both, and after I listened to them, it hit me so hard because of the way they explained what they went through. It made me feel so blessed because I could have been there. I know many times while I was in the world that God spared my life. I believe it was because of my father's and mother's many prayers that I wasn't killed.

But what hit me the most was how I heard about people dying or getting killed on the news just about every day and thinking about where they may end up. After listening to those videos, I could not shake what I was feeling because the feeling was so strong. I learned so much from listening to their testimonies, and though I was grateful before I watched them, I must say that now, I am way beyond way more grateful to God!

I want to encourage everyone to listen to these videos so that you can be grateful that you are alive, but mostly so that you can have a heart to not only pray for souls to be saved but for God to send laborers to the lost. I encourage you to send these videos to people you know and have them send them to people they know. Some people may be shy about witnessing to other people, but thank God that we have great technology!

As we continue to pray and seek God's Word, we will be filled with God's power so that we can overcome sin. Remember God's words are Spirit and life, and His words are also the power of God. We were all born into sin, and it will take time for us to get cleaned up.

Don't ever let the devil keep reminding you of that sin that you have asked for forgiveness for! The devil will always and forever keep telling you that you are not forgiven. As long as we are breathing, we can always ask God for forgiveness. But we must believe His Word, which says that He will forgive us and cleanse us from all unrighteousness, and we must always be thankful to God for His great mercy and for His forgiveness.

God takes His time working in us to perfection just as a great painter takes his time when he paints a beautiful picture! If they didn't take their time, then the picture would pretty much just be junk! Though we hear that God never made junk when He created man, they forget to mention that we became junk when Adam and Eve disobeyed God.

I thank God that He didn't give up on us! God sent His Son to a junkyard planet in order to refurbish us! We must believe that "we are His workmanship, created in Christ Jesus unto good works which God had before ordained that we should walk in them" (Ephesians 2:10). That means that He is working in us! We all must be patient with what He is doing in us and thank Him for being so patient with us.

When I feel the excruciating sharp pains of being carved by God, I tell Him to go ahead and carve away! I know that I shall be complete in Jesus! Even though we have all come short of His glory, we can be sure that we are going from glory to glory! "But we all, with open face beholding as in a glass the glory of the Lord, are change into the same image from glory to glory even as by the Spirit of the Lord" (2 Corinthians 3:18).

I know that I am getting closer to His glory each and every day, and I can confidently say that I can truly feel the glory of God in me more than ever! It's amazing! God wants all of us to experience His glory, and as you continue seeking God, you will be able to experience His awesome glory too!

Chapter 24

There Is Power in the Word

As I have been seeking God on a daily basis, I can say that I have felt God's presence mightily, and that's all good, but I knew that I was still missing something. It wasn't till later on that I realized that one very important thing that I was lacking in my life was for me to speak God's Word over my situations. It seemed like every time that something bad would happen, I would always find myself looking to get prayer from someone else for my situations.

I realized that I rarely spoke God's Word over my situations. When my mom got sick in her body, as stated before, I would completely lose it! I would pray and cry and beg God to heal her until I realized that I was missing the main ingredient for her healing, which was speaking and confessing God's Word over my situations.

As I stated before, God is the Word, and when we have the Word in us, then we actually have God in us. So, when I began speaking God's Word over my mom was when she would get healed. I had mentioned when my mom started talking out of her mind. I felt that spirit of dementia trying to take over her, and of course, I went downright crazy, but then I began speaking God's Word and binding that spirit off her, and immediately she came to her right mind.

It wasn't a day later or a month later, but it was immediately! My thoughts were, *Wow! I could have had a V8!* The Bible says the Word of God is quick and powerful, but I didn't realize that the Word was that quick, or maybe I just didn't believe! I must say that it took practice for me to continue to speak God's Word over my situations, just as it took practice for me to take time to pray and study God's Word.

Sadly, there are so many distractions that get in our way of doing what will help us live to the fullest in Christ Jesus. There have been times that I have had experiences where God was completely taking over me. I would feel His faith working in me, and I would feel His confidence in me, and I would even feel His boldness. Then there were times when I would feel like Peter when he was walking on the water, and I would see the waves crashing and would begin to sink! Distraction...distraction...distraction!

The devil also uses words in order to get us off focus, and he never stops talking...ever! When a person hears something over and over again, after a while they tend to believe what they hear. Sadly, sometimes the devil only has to say something one time, and he will get people to believe what he is saying. When he spoke to Eve in the garden of Eden, he knew that if he kept talking to her, she would eventually believe what he was saying.

When the devil talks, he can be so convincing, and sometimes he just makes so much sense. If we are not careful and we don't have God's Word inside of us, then it will not be hard to believe the devil's word. We must remember that the devil is a father of lies and every word that he says is a lie!

When we get sick, he tells us that we are going to die! He will tell you that you will not be able to pay your bills, you are going to lose your job, your spouse is cheating on you, you're going to fail, and the list goes on and on and on. I'm finding out that even though there are bad things happening today, I can still use God's Word against whatever bad thing may be happening.

You may have been told that you have a few months to live. When you have God's Word in you, faith will arise, and you can move mighty mountains (Matthew 17:20). The Bible says, "Who hath believed our report?" (Isaiah 53:1). God's words are life, and Satan's words are death.

When the Bible says that death and life are in the power of our tongue, it means what it says and says what it means! Whatever words that we choose to speak can cause death or life. In Genesis 1 we read that in the beginning, nothing was until God said or spoke it. The Spirit was there, but nothing got done until God spoke, and then things were formed and created.

We must also remember the Word of God is Spirit, and God is a Spirit. They are One. Once again, when we have God's Word in us, then we have God in us. Can you really comprehend that? God is in us! In the beginning was the Word, and the Word was made flesh; if you abide in me and my words abide in you...

As I spoke previously on the effects that negative words can have on people, and when we speak God's words over people, that will also have an impact on other people's lives. We can actually speak life over people. The Bible tells us to pray for our enemies for a reason.

I stated before that it is not God's will for any person to perish, but His desires are for everyone to repent and to have everlasting life. When I was in the world, I had my share of enemies, and sadly, I also had many enemies in the church I attended! I would not have minded for them to pray for me and speak life over me instead of cursing me.

Even though that may not be easy for people to do, not even for a saved person, when we see through God's eyes and feel God's love, then it won't be so hard for us to do. God sent His only Son to die for us while we were living in our sin, and He died a horrific death on the cross for each and every one of us. No one was left out!

> *For as rain cometh down, and the snow from heaven and returneth not thither, but watereth the earth, and maketh it bring forth and bud, that it may give seed to the sower and bread to the eater: so shall my Word be that goeth forth out of my mouth: it shall not return unto me void, but it shall accomplish that which I please, and it shall prosper in the thing whereto I send it.*
>
> Isaiah 55:10–11

We really have to be able to comprehend that Jesus is the Word of God, and the Word is Spirit, and the same Spirit that raised Christ from the dead is now living inside of us! And we must remember to speak His Word in order to activate His divine power! We have been given the authority to do what Jesus did as we allow God to completely take control of our lives. Devils will recognize when we speak with authority, but don't forget that they also recognize when we do not have any authority whatsoever!

> *Then certain of the vagabond Jews, exorcists, took upon them to call over them which had evil spirits the name of the Lord Jesus, saying, We adjure you by Jesus whom Paul preacheth. And there were seven sons of one Sceva, a Jew, and chief of the priests, which did so. And the evil spirit answered and said, Jesus I know, and Paul I know; but who are ye? And the man in whom the evil spirit was leaped on them, and overcame them, and prevailed against them, so that they fled out of that house naked and wounded.*
>
> Acts 19:13–16

When we have God in us and are doing what God wants us to do, then God will be the One speaking through us. He will be doing the healing, casting out devils, and not we ourselves. We are just a vessel that He will use to accomplish His work. I so long to see the days when the earth is shining ever so brightly with sons and daughters of God who are living in victory and with power!

I believe that it will be just a matter of time! I will continue to speak, "Thy kingdom come; Thy will be done on earth as it is in heaven!"

Chapter 25

There Is Freedom in Forgiveness

When I was living for the devil, I loved to hate, and I hated to love. I didn't trust anyone, and I loved very few people. One being my mother of course: I love her dearly! I also love my father very much, but I must admit that I didn't love him like I love my mom because of the way that he raised me. He was very strict, and as I said earlier, he followed a bunch of people who called themselves Christians! They were heartless, and their goal was to make other people follow a bunch of man-made rules that they did not follow themselves!

They were a bunch of hypocrites who condemned anyone who didn't obey them! Before my dad got hooked on their religion, when he showed up to their church, the pastor of the church would be waiting at the door to greet everyone, and he would say, "Here comes the devil!" and he would say it right in front of my mom! My dad would just smile and go and sit in the church with all of us!

Wouldn't you know that same pastor who called my father the devil ended up leaving his wife and taking off with the organ player! So once my family was of age, we all went our separate ways and pretty much lived totally opposite of the way we were raised up. We did not like church an ounce bit!

We partied hard, and we lived like there was no tomorrow! We really didn't know any better because we were not raised according to the truth of the Bible. My dad and mom tried their best to raise us up the right way, but sadly it wasn't the right way. I believe that it took my father's and mother's continual prayers to bring most of us back to God.

Because of this religion, we never received the proper love from my father. Instead, we lived a life of abnormality and were tortured by his religion! My dad learned what he learned from a preacher! He listened to them way too many times! We were never told about the fruits of the Spirit because, basically, there were no fruits whatsoever in the churches that we had attended!

The only thing that I had experienced in these churches in my early years was being around stuck-up, snooty, self-righteous, ruthless people who thought they were all that! They never would talk to my mom, and when they would talk to my dad, it would be about tithing! They always treated us like we were beneath them.

The church had a school, and my dad sent two of my siblings and me there, where we were all ridiculed by the teachers. It was the school of the spirit all right, but not God's Spirit! Some of our teachers were demonic and so full of hatred for us. I remember one time when one of those teachers took my notebook from me, and let me tell you that there was some bad stuff in there!

I wrote a lot of things about them in my notebook and was full of nothing but hatred. I can tell you that there were not many good words in it. My little brother, who attended this school, tried to get my notebook away from that teacher, but the teacher had a good grip on it, and he wouldn't let it go. So my little brother punched him in the nose!

That was the first time that I had experienced the fruit of the Spirit because joy and laughter came over me when that happened! The joy of the Lord is my strength! LOL! This is one of the teachers who hated my siblings and me! He would punish us in any way that he could.

One time the school planned a trip to go to Six Flags, and this teacher said that my siblings and I could not go. I don't exactly remember his reasons, but he refused to let us go. What was very upsetting was that we had to attend church every Wednesday night, and he would be the one giving the sermon! "Preach, preacher!"

Well, he ended up dying at an early age, and even on his deathbed, he gave instructions to the school staff for them not to allow us to go to Six Flags! I hated being at that school so much that I tried to kill myself. That was when I started loving to hate. I didn't receive this from the world, but I got this hate from the so-called church! I guess you could say that I became like them. Hallelujah! I became one mean, hard-core machine!

Sadly, even today so many people experience this kind of thing at churches! This hatred followed me most of my life only because that was all that I knew. When I started living for the world, I realized that there was no difference except for the fact that I had fun in the world! I loved dancing, and I loved getting drunk! I partied seven days a week!

But I thank God that I ended up running into a dead end and I gave my life to God before it was too late! Once I gave my life to God, immediately I began to experience joy, peace, and happiness for the first time in my life. It was real all right, but I still didn't know much about this God thing and how to live it out.

So I ended up going to a church that taught me a lot. Unfortunately, I experienced the same kind of treatment in this church from their so-called leaders there as I had experienced at the other churches that my dad raised me in. Then I realized that the devils are churchgoers, and many of them are leaders in the church!

These churchgoers were also snooty and snobby, and they thought that they were all that as well! They were self-centered, self-righteous people who were there to make you a slave to them or get you out of the church! I must say that they went to digging plenty of pits for me to fall in!

The devils don't need to go to the bars because they got those people already. So, when I began going through my trials, then all these feelings of hatred popped up. I hated everybody! I wished them dead as well as myself! My sleep meds looked really good at that time, and I mean the whole bottle! I just wanted to sleep away. Once again, I was miserable!

I was so full of anger, and when people did things for me, it was never enough! I would be so upset because they didn't do more for me, and boy, did I ever let them know it! People hurt me so much, and there was nothing that anyone could say to make me feel any other way than to hate until I began to read the Bible through.

When I did that, I began to understand about people who hurt other people. Not only that, but I began to see myself and how I hurt so many people. I began to see myself and how I was just like the people who did me wrong. I didn't realize that I was hurting the people that I hurt. I didn't even mean to hurt anyone. I was blind!

Saul of Tarsus didn't mean to hurt God's people. He even believed that he was doing God's work because that was what the religious people told him! But when I began reading the Bible, then I began to see. I read that we were all born in darkness or in sin. God's Word is the light that will reveal our darkness or dark ways, and it will take us from darkness into His marvelous light if we allow it to.

When Jesus called Saul, he blinded him and then gave him the commission. "To open their eyes, and to turn them from darkness to light, and from the power of Satan unto God, that they may receive forgiveness of sins, and inheritance among them which are sanctified by faith that is in me" (Acts 26:18). "Then spake Jesus again unto them, saying, I am the light of the world: he that followeth me shall not walk in darkness, but shall have the light of life" (John 8:12).

"For God, who commanded the light to shine out of darkness, hath shined in our hearts, to give the light of the knowledge of the glory of God in the face of Jesus Christ" (2 Corinthians 4:6). "Open thou mine eyes, that I may behold wondrous things out of thy law" (Psalm 119:18).

As I stated before, only God can open the blind eyes, and the way God opens our eyes is through His Word. After all, He is the light of the world! When I realized how much hate I was carrying, I didn't know how I was going to get rid of it. I was never fond of the scriptures that talked about love. Those scriptures would literally make me cringe! That's how much hate I was carrying.

I knew that I could not ignore those scriptures anymore. Even though I had every excuse to hate the people whom I hated, I knew that wasn't going to get me to heaven. So, once again, I had to go to God with this and be real. I had to be truthful. I didn't go to God and tell Him that I loved the people whom I hated, but I went to God and told Him that I hated the people whom I hated and that I wanted them to die and burn in hell! Just being real!

I would pray to God to help me forgive those people and to help me pray for them. I can say that it didn't happen overnight, but it took years for me to finally forgive, just as it did for me to stop lying. God began doing a healing process in my heart from the pain that was deeply rooted in me. When He began healing me, then I began to see a little light, and as time went by, the light would appear brighter and brighter.

I was coming out of darkness and slowly going toward His marvelous light. The Bible says, "The light of the body is the eye: if therefore thine eye be single, thy whole body shall be full of light. But if thine eye be evil, thy whole body shall be full of darkness. If therefore the light that is in thee be darkness, how great is that darkness!" (Mathew 6:22–23).

I had been living in total darkness, and I felt like my whole body was too. I wanted revenge! I wanted my enemies to really suffer in a bad way! I wanted God to strike them dead! What was crazy was when I saw my enemies, I could feel that darkness in my whole being.

After I asked God to help me with this, I began to notice a change as with everything else. I knew that it was God working in me for sure! Then, after a while, I was able to pray for the people who hurt me, and when I did that, God began to show me that those people can't see and that they are living in darkness as I once was.

After a while, I began to feel the weight of hatred lift off from me, and I could feel myself coming out of a very dark place as I was moving toward God's marvelous light! Then I began to experience the real joy of the Lord and the peace of God that passes all understanding. Now when I look at someone who is miserable, it's not hard for me to see that they are walking in darkness. Now instead of me getting upset with someone for what they do to hurt me, I feel sorry for them.

When we are walking in the light, then we will be able to brighten other people's day. I remember one time when I was walking outside, I saw this woman looking for the gym at the apartment building where we were living. She wasn't very happy, and she was using a lot of vulgarity. I just listened to her, and then I started talking to her.

My sister Abby showed up, and she started talking to her also. She told us that no one at our apartment had ever said a word to her and that we were the first people to ever speak to her. My sister invited her to church, and she didn't answer, but then after a few weeks went by, she told us that she had decided to go with us!

So we took her to church, and she said that she really enjoyed it! Her face lit up, and she said that she loved the service! We had such a good time! It was amazing how her countenance changed. We later found out that her son was suicidal, and she was really struggling with that. If we want to be the light of the world, then we must let go of the darkness.

Unforgiveness and hatred will keep us in total darkness, and it will also keep us in total bondage. It is such a miserable feeling! It wasn't easy for me to let go, but if I had known that I could have been this free a long time ago, I would have done this a long time ago! Hatred is not worth me living in total darkness and misery.

I realized that the people whom I hated moved on and could care less that I hated them, so why would I continue to allow myself to suffer for them? I was the only one being affected by hating other people. The reason it took me years to let go was that I was a very hateful person for many, many years.

We should not allow our enemies to dictate how we should feel. People come, and people go, and you can be sure that offenses will always come. We can see that the world is getting darker, and we should not allow people who are living in darkness to put our light out. It's just not worth it! Most of all, they are not worth our salvation.

Jesus is the light of the world, and once again, Jesus tells us that we must let our light shine so that God will get the glory. When Jesus was on the cross, He said, "Father, forgive them; for they know not what they do" (Luke 23:34). If He forgave His enemies who crucified Him, then for us to forgive someone who has caused us pain can't be compared to the pain that He suffered.

God is love, and when we have perfect love, the Bible tells us that we won't fear. "There is no fear in love; but perfect love casteth out fear: because fear hath torment. He that feareth is not made perfect in love" (1 John 4:18). There will always be people who will hate us, whether it be for our faith or not; that's just a part of life.

The other day I went outside and saw my car messed up on each side. I kind of giggled only because my car doesn't mean that much to me for me to have a cow over it! I have no idea who did it and probably never will. Jesus was hated, mocked, and even killed, but He knew the freedom in forgiveness. It's such a great feeling to be free!

The Conclusion

What I have learned is priceless! For many years I felt like I was just existing. I knew that there had to be more to this life than what I was feeling. I knew that God was way more than what I was experiencing, and with God's help I was able to experience God in a way that I never dreamed of!

One thing is to experience God, and another thing is to know the God that you are experiencing. Many people can say that they have experienced God in a way like none other, and they may have, but experiencing God does not bring the knowledge of God. The closer that we get to God, the closer that He will get to us. The problem is that people believe that they are okay with the way things are until they really need God to show up as I did.

It was either God showed up or I was hitting the bars and drinking myself silly! With all the experiences that I had with God and with all the manifestations that I felt when God touched me, and even with all the dreams and visitations that I had from God, it still wasn't enough when this trial came along. I cannot begin to tell you the experience that I had been through with God when I chose to seek Him like never before!

Sometimes what happened to me feels like a dream, and when I think about what happened, I begin to relive the realness of it. God showed up in a most powerful way, and there's no denying what I have experienced. God is so real to me that when I read the Bible, I can actually visualize what's in it happening. And when I read about God's greatness and His power, it's like I'm there with Him, and my faith gets lifted every time that I read about my King.

God is not a man, but He is a God who desires to be worshipped. People so mistake God for a man and, therefore, don't believe what the Bible says about Him in the Old Testament is what God really did. Until we know that God in the New Testament is the same God in the Old Testament and understand that He never changes, then people will be partial in their way of thinking about Him.

I would live my life trying to become like someone else, but all the time God was trying to get my attention so that He could make me be the person who He had created me to be, and it wasn't somebody else either! He is our designer, and He has designed each and every one of us to be different, but sadly people may feel like because they are not like the uppity up, the Joneses, or the self-righteous that they are worthless. That's so far from the truth!

My mom always felt that way about herself and growing up and I felt that way about myself for a very long time. So I felt like I had to act, walk, and even talk like those who looked important and looked like they had it all together! God has placed something inside of us all that He wants to bring out of us in order to display His glory and in order for us to impact the people around us!

So many people are satisfied of what they have experienced with God, but God has no limits of what He can show us. He wants to be so close to us. He wants to show us so much more than we could ever imagine! And He wants to be the potter of our lives and create something beautiful!

God will take our fears and make us bolder than a lion. He wants to take our insecurities and help us to be confident in Him. He wants to take our frustrations and give us His peace that passes all understanding. He wants us to walk in great faith knowing that no matter what situations we may be facing, He will bring us through victoriously! He wants us to do what Jesus did and greater works! But He needs our time and our undivided attention for us to do these things.

When you let go of what you may think that things should be like, then God will take you under His wings, and you will begin to fly and see the world in a whole different way, unimaginable! Not only that—you will be able to live the life that God intended for you to live and be the person that God intended for you to be. When I look in the mirror, I don't see anybody else, but I see the person who God intended me to be. I see meeee! "Nevertheless, I live, yet not I, but Christ liveth in me!" (Galatians 2:20).

Milton Keynes UK
Ingram Content Group UK Ltd.
UKHW031617231124
451036UK00003B/38